THE
GREEN
AIR FRYER
COOKBOOK

THE
GREEN
AIR FRYER
COOKBOOK

80 QUICK AND TASTY VEGAN AND VEGETARIAN RECIPES

DENISE SMART

hamlyn

hamlyn

First published in Great Britain
in 2023 by Hamlyn, an imprint of
Octopus Publishing Group Ltd
Carmelite House
50 Victoria Embankment
London EC4Y 0DZ
www.octopusbooks.co.uk

An Hachette UK Company
www.hachette.co.uk

Some of this material previously appeared in *Hamlyn All Colour Cookery: 200 Air Fryer Recipes*.

Distributed in the US by Hachette Book Group
1290 Avenue of the Americas
4th and 5th Floors
New York, NY 10104

Distributed in Canada by Canadian Manda Group
664 Annette St., Toronto
Ontario, Canada M6S 2C8

ISBN 978-0-600-63827-8

A CIP catalogue record for this book is available from the British Library.

Printed and bound in China

10 9 8 7 6 5 4 3 2 1

Standard level spoon measurement are used in all recipes.
1 tablespoon = one 15 ml spoon
1 teaspoon = one 5 ml spoon

Eggs should be medium unless otherwise stated. The Department of Health advises that eggs should not be consumed raw. This book contains dishes made with raw or lightly cooked eggs. It is prudent for more vulnerable people such as pregnant and nursing mothers, the elderly, babies and young children to avoid uncooked or lightly cooked dishes made with eggs. Once prepared these dishes should be kept refrigerated and used promptly.

Milk should be full fat unless otherwise stated.

Fresh herbs should be used unless otherwise stated. If unavailable use dried herbs as an alternative but halve the quantities stated.

Pepper should be freshly ground black pepper unless otherwise stated.

This book includes dishes made with nuts and nut derivatives. It is advisable for those with known allergic reactions to nuts and nut derivatives and those who may be potentially vulnerable to these allergies, to avoid dishes made with nuts and nut oils. It is also prudent to check the labels of pre-prepared ingredients for the possible inclusion of nut derivatives.

Vegetarians should look for the 'V' symbol on a cheese to ensure it is made with vegetarian rennet.

CONTENTS

INTRODUCTION

If you've purchased this book, you are probably already the proud owner of an air fryer – the must-have kitchen appliance that everyone is talking about.

This book will show you exactly why air fryers have become so popular. Rest assured, this is not just another impulsive purchase that you will eventually tire of and pack away in the back of a cupboard. Affordable, energy-efficient and easy, air fryers can revolutionize your kitchen experience. These handy gadgets use less energy and oil and take less time than conventional ovens, helping you prepare fuss-free versions of all your favourite dishes.

Whether you are a beginner wishing to learn more, or an experienced air fryer user seeking fresh inspiration, this cookbook will show you how to get the most out of this amazing appliance.

The book contains 80 easy-to-prepare sweet and savoury dishes, suitable for every occasion. All of the recipes use easily sourced ingredients and are guaranteed to make the process of preparing and cooking food in your air fryer simple and successful. In the following pages, you will find delicious ideas for breakfast, easy speedy mains, light bites and sides, and sweet treats.

WHAT IS AN AIR FRYER?

An air fryer is basically a small oven. The name is deceptive because it is not a traditional 'fryer' as we know it, but it cooks food in a way that achieves that same fried effect.

Air fryers contain a heating element located at the top, which is enhanced by a powerful fan. The fan circulates the hot air around the food, which sits on a removable crisping plate. Air fryers typically heat up and cook food very quickly and evenly, thanks to the concentrated heat source as well as the size and position of the fan. Because of their well-balanced time and temperature controls, air fryers produce perfect food that is juicy, crispy and delicious.

WHICH IS THE BEST AIR FRYER FOR ME?

There are many air fryers on the market – the range can be mind-boggling for the first-time buyer. However, there are several factors you can consider to help you narrow down your selection.

First, take into account the different functions. Many air fryers have pre-set programmes for meat, fish, vegetables and frozen foods. Some models have a 'shake' function, which reminds you to shake the basket or turn the food halfway through the cooking time. Others have a 'keep warm' function. Some air fryers have a single drawer, while others have dual drawers that allow you to cook different foods at different temperatures at the same time, or cook a main and a side simultaneously. Consider which features and functions are most appealing for your household.

The second factor to take into consideration is how many people you are cooking for as different air fryers have different capacities. The smallest air fryers (1–2 litres/quarts) are suitable for 1–2 people, the medium sizes (3–4 litres/quarts) are good for 2–3 people, and the largest (6 litres/quarts or more) are perfect if you are cooking for 4–6 people.

Finally, you need to take note of how much room you have in your kitchen, as some models can take up a lot of worktop space.

The recipes in this book were prepared in a 5 litre (5 quart) air fryer with a single drawer.

WHAT ARE THE BENEFITS OF AN AIR FRYER?

Air fryers are much healthier Traditional frying methods use lots of oil. However, with an air fryer, you can make foods like chips and doughnuts with only 1–2 teaspoons of oil.

Air fryers are energy efficient Because they are smaller than conventional ovens, air fryers heat up quicker and cook food faster, which could save you money on your electricity bills.

Air fryers are quicker Although you may occasionally need to cook in batches (depending on the size of your appliance), overall, having an air fryer will save you time in the kitchen. In general, air fryers reduce cooking times by about 20 per cent.

Air fryers are perfect for small-batch bakes Because of their size, these appliances lend themselves well to baking small batches of cakes, cookies and other sweet treats.

Air fryers are great for reheating Whereas microwaving can make certain foods go soggy, air fryers allow you to reheat your meals and still retain that delicious, crispy crunch.

Air fryers are amazing for cooking frozen foods Conventional ovens can often dry out frozen foods but air fryers are perfect for cooking foods like frozen chips and potato wedges.

Air fryers are fuss-free appliances Unlike traditional ovens, an air fryer will not heat up your whole kitchen, and it will lessen the intensity of cooking smells. Using an air fryer also means you have minimal clean up at the end as it will all be contained within the drawer.

DO I NEED ANY SPECIAL EQUIPMENT?

The simple answer is no, but you might consider using the following equipment to make your air frying experience even easier:

- Small metal baking tins, 17 cm (6½ inches) square and up to 20 cm (8 inches) round, depending on the size of your air fryer.

- Small ovenproof dishes, ramekins and small metal pudding tins.

- Spray bottles for oil. Some of the recipes in this book recommend spritzing your food with oil to make it crispy.

- Pastry brush, for brushing oil and glazing the surfaces of food.

- Perforated silicone liners or mats for air fryers. Alternatively, you can simply pierce holes in pieces of nonstick baking paper, although remember never to place these in your air fryer without any food on top as they could fly into the fan element and catch fire.

- Rubber-tipped heatproof tongs, for turning food. These also prevent you from scratching the tray.

- Foil, for covering food. This prevents food with longer cooking times from becoming too brown.

- Mandolin, for making evenly sized, thin slices of fruits and vegetables.

- Small metal, wooden or bamboo skewers that fit in your air fryer. If using wood or bamboo, remember to soak them in water first.

TIPS FOR USING YOUR AIR FRYER

- Always read the manufacturer's instructions before using your new air fryer. This will help you operate your appliance properly and safely, and will ensure you get the best out of your air fryer.

- The recipes in this book specify standard oven cooking temperatures. Some air fryers come with less standard temperatures, so just choose the closest setting to the temperature specified. For example, your air fryer may have 199°C (390°F) instead of 200°C (400°F). Like ovens, different models might cook slightly hotter or cooler. This means you may have to adjust the cooking time by a minute or so. Be mindful of this slight variation, and take the time to get to know your own model beforehand.

- Most of the recipes in this book recommend shaking or turning the food partway through cooking for an even cook. The benefit of the air fryer is that you can open the drawer and check how the food is cooking without all the heat escaping, especially during the last few minutes.

- To reduce cooking times even further, always preheat the air fryer to the temperature recommended in the recipes.

- Cut vegetables into even-sized pieces so they cook at the same rate.

- Always cook food in a single layer. Never overcrowd the drawer, or your food will cook unevenly and take more time. Air fryers work by circulating air around food, so they require a little space.

- You will still require a little oil to cook most foods, especially breaded foods, so consider filling a small spray bottle with oil to help you achieve that perfect, crispy crumb.

- Cover dishes with foil to prevent the food from becoming too brown. This is especially useful for larger cakes and quiches.

- Clean your appliance after every use. Air fryers are very easy to clean with hot soapy water.

- Never fill your appliance with oil – it is not a deep fryer.

THE BEST FOODS FOR AIR FRYING

- **Potatoes** – chips (homemade or frozen), whole baked potatoes, wedges, roast
- **Vegetables** – cauliflower, carrots, parsnips, courgettes, peppers, aubergines
- **Pastry** – shortcrust, puff, filo
- **Fruit** – stone fruits (such as peaches, apricots and mangoes), pineapple, apples, bananas

FOODS TO AVOID

- **Uncoated popcorn or popcorn kernels** – they may fly into the element and cause damage
- **Wet, saucy foods** – foods with lots of sauce, such as stews, or foods coated in drippy batter don't cook well in an air fryer. Dry spice rubs, glazes and dried breadcrumbs work best
- **Rice, pasta and pulses** – dry foods that need to soften as they boil in water should not be cooked in an air fryer

STORE CUPBOARD AND FREEZER ESSENTIALS

Below are some of the most commonly used ingredients in the recipes:

- **Oils** – olive oil, sunflower oil and flavoured oils, such as chilli and garlic
- **Dried breadcrumbs** – fine and panko
- **Dried herbs** – mixed herbs, oregano, rosemary and thyme
- **Dried garlic and onion powder**
- **Spices** – paprika, ground cinnamon, ginger, turmeric, cumin and chilli
- **Ready-prepared spice mixes** – Moroccan, Middle Eastern and Mexican
- **Pastes** – harissa, vegetarian or vegan pesto, gochujang, miso and chipotle
- **Nuts** – almonds, walnuts, pecans and pine nuts
- **Dried fruits** – apricots, mixed tropical fruit and dates

- **Seeds** – sesame, pumpkin, sunflower and linseed
- **Flours** – plain, self-raising, cornflour and baking powder
- **Sugars** – caster, granulated, soft brown, honey and maple syrup
- **Sauces** – sweet chilli, ketchup and soy sauce
- **Frozen foods** – peas, frozen chips and fries

WHAT MAKES THIS COOKBOOK 'GREEN'?

Most people associate frying with chips, meat or fish. However, this cookbook will show you that your air fryer can make so much more. *The Green Air Fryer Cookbook* contains an equal number of tasty vegetarian and vegan recipes in every chapter, perfect for those who are transitioning from vegetarianism to veganism, those who switch between the two dietary preferences regularly, or even meat-eaters who are just looking to incorporate more vegetables into their diet.

PLANT-BASED DIETS

Many people choose to follow a vegetarian or vegan diet for religious, social, lifestyle, moral, environmental or health reasons, but what is the difference between them?

The Vegetarian Society defines a vegetarian as 'Someone who lives on a diet of grains, pulses, nuts, seeds, vegetables and fruits with, or without, the use of dairy products and eggs. A vegetarian does not eat any meat, poultry, game, fish, shellfish or by-products of slaughter.'

The Vegan Society states that 'Veganism is a philosophy and way of living which seeks to exclude – as far as is possible and practicable – all forms of exploitation of, and cruelty to, animals for food, clothing or any other purpose. In dietary terms it denotes the practice of dispensing with all products derived wholly or partly from animals.'

Vegan diets have become very popular in recent years and focus on foods primarily from plants. This includes not only fruits and vegetables, but also nuts, seeds, oils, whole grains, legumes and beans.

Today, being a vegan or vegetarian is so much easier. Supermarkets and health food stores are full of produce to help you cook inspirational and tasty dishes. Vegan and vegetarian alternatives are now readily available, and foods are clearly labelled with the vegetarian or vegan symbol. However, remember to check the labels on the foods you buy. For example, gelatine may be used in some manufactured products, and rennet may be used in the cheese-making process. Likewise, some curry pastes may contain shrimp and vegetable stock is not always vegan.

Vegan or vegetarian cooking is sometimes seen as bland or time-consuming. This book aims to dispel this myth by providing delicious and exciting recipes to help you create simple, flavourful food to cook in your air fryer, in a fraction of the time, using both fresh and store cupboard ingredients.

IT'S TIME TO GET COOKING!

The recipes in this book will inspire you to get creative – whether it's for one, two, or for the whole family – so get started by picking one of the delicious choices and giving it a try. It's amazing what you can create with fresh vegetables and store cupboard ingredients and, as air frying is a healthier way of cooking, you will be able to enjoy well-balanced meals in a fraction of the time. The more you cook with it, the more you will discover inventive ways to use your air fryer. Remember, because it's portable, this appliance can also be used away from home on staycations.

Like many air fryer owners, you will soon find that you can't wait to tell your friends and family about all the tasty dishes you've created from just a few simple ingredients.

Happy air frying!

 VEGETARIAN

 VEGAN

BREAKFAST CLUB

MAKES 6
Preparation time 15 minutes
Cooking time 20 minutes

APRICOT & ALMOND PASTRIES

125 g (4 oz) mascarpone cheese
25 g (1 oz) icing sugar
50 g (2 oz) ground almonds
½ teaspoon almond extract
1 sheet of ready-rolled puff
    pastry
beaten egg, to glaze
6 apricot halves, fresh or from
    a can, drained
25 g (1 oz) flaked almonds
2 tablespoons apricot jam

Place the mascarpone, icing sugar, ground almonds and almond extract in a bowl and mix well.

Unroll the puff pastry and cut it into 6 squares, about 10 cm (4 inches) across. Divide the almond mixture equally between the squares, spreading it out slightly but leaving a 1 cm (½ inch) border on all sides. Brush the edges of the pastry with a little beaten egg, then lift 2 opposite corners of one of the pastries and pinch together, before repeating with the other 2 corners, to make a parcel.

Push down in the centre of the parcel to make a well and pop an apricot half on top. Repeat with the remaining pastries. Brush the pastries with egg and sprinkle over the flaked almonds.

Cook half the pastries in a preheated air fryer at 180°C (350°F) for 9–10 minutes, until risen and golden and the bases are crispy. Repeat with the remaining pastries.

Warm the jam, then brush over the tops of the pastries to glaze. Serve warm or cold.

SERVES 2
Preparation time 2 minutes
Cooking time 8 minutes

SOFT-BOILED EGGS & SOLDIERS

2 eggs
2 slices of bread
butter, for spreading
salt and pepper

Place the eggs in their shells in a preheated air fryer and cook at 180°C (350°F) for 6 minutes. Remove and place in egg cups.

Cook the bread in the air fryer for 1 minute, then turn over and cook the other side for a further minute, until lightly toasted. Spread with the butter and cut into fingers.

Cut the tops off the eggs, season to taste and serve with the toast soldiers for dipping.

SERVES 4–6
Preparation time 10 minutes
Cooking time 30 minutes

BANANA BREAKFAST LOAF

3 tablespoons olive or sunflower oil, plus extra for greasing
2 tablespoons honey
1 egg, beaten
2 ripe bananas, mashed
3 tablespoons buttermilk or natural yogurt
75 g (3 oz) plain flour
75 g (3 oz) spelt or wholemeal flour
½ teaspoon bicarbonate of soda
½ teaspoon baking powder
1 teaspoon ground mixed spice
1 tablespoon chia seeds
50 g (2 oz) pitted dates, chopped
50 g (2 oz) pecans, roughly chopped

To serve
natural yogurt
mixed berries, such as raspberries and blueberries

Grease and line the base of a 500 g (1 lb) loaf tin or an 18 cm (7 inch) round cake tin, 7 cm (3 inches) deep, with nonstick baking paper.

Whisk together the oil, honey, egg, bananas and buttermilk in a large bowl. Sift over the flours, bicarbonate of soda, baking powder and mixed spice. Stir until combined, then stir in the chia seeds, dates and pecans, until well combined. Spoon into the prepared tin.

Cook in a preheated air fryer at 150°C (300°F) for 30 minutes, until golden brown and risen and a skewer inserted into the middle comes out clean.

Cool in the tin for a few minutes, then turn out on to a wire rack to cool completely before serving in slices with yogurt and fresh berries.

SERVES 2
Preparation time 10 minutes
Cooking time 15 minutes

SWEET POTATO & SPRING ONION FRITTERS WITH AVOCADO

1 sweet potato, peeled and
   coarsely grated
4 spring onions, chopped
2 tablespoons chopped chives
50 g (2 oz) self-raising flour
1 egg, lightly beaten
olive oil, for spritzing
salt and pepper

To serve
sunflower oil, for frying
2 eggs
1 avocado, stoned, peeled
   and sliced

Squeeze the grated sweet potato in a clean tea towel to remove excess water, then place in a large bowl. Add the spring onions, chives and flour, then stir in the egg. Mix well and season with salt and pepper.

Divide the mixture into 4 and use your hands to shape into flat patties. Place in a preheated air fryer, spritz with olive oil and cook at 190°C (375°F) for 8 minutes. Flip over, spritz with a little more oil and cook for a further 6–7 minutes, until golden.

When the fritters are nearly cooked, heat a little sunflower oil in a frying pan, crack in the eggs and fry to your liking.

Serve 2 fritters per person, each topped with half the sliced avocado and a fried egg. Sprinkle with a good grind of black pepper.

SERVES 2
Preparation time 5 minutes
Cooking time 16 minutes

SHAKSHUKA WITH FETA

1 red onion, sliced

1 small red pepper, cored, deseeded and thinly sliced

2 teaspoons olive oil

¼ teaspoon smoked chilli flakes

50 g (2 oz) vegetarian feta cheese, crumbled

2 eggs

1 tablespoon chopped flat leaf parsley

crusty bread, to serve

Tomato sauce

250 g (8 oz) canned chopped tomatoes

1 tablespoon tomato ketchup

1 garlic clove, crushed

½ teaspoon ground cumin

½ teaspoon ground coriander

½ teaspoon smoked hot paprika

salt and pepper

Place the onion, red pepper, olive oil and chilli flakes in an ovenproof dish or tin. Stir well, place the dish in a preheated air fryer and cook at 180°C (350°F) for 10 minutes, stirring halfway through.

Meanwhile, combine all the sauce ingredients together in a bowl. When the vegetables have finished cooking, pour over the sauce and stir well.

Stir in half the feta, then make 2 wells in the mixture and crack in the eggs. Return to the air fryer and cook for a further 5–6 minutes, or until the eggs are just set.

Sprinkle over the remaining feta and parsley and a good grind of black pepper. Serve immediately with crusty bread.

MAKES 12
Preparation time 10 minutes
Cooking time 16 minutes

ICED CINNAMON ROLLS

1 tablespoon ground cinnamon
3 tablespoons caster sugar
1 sheet of ready-rolled puff
    pastry
1 egg, beaten

Icing
50 g (2 oz) icing sugar
1–2 teaspoons cold water

Mix the cinnamon and caster sugar in a small bowl. Unroll the pastry sheet and sprinkle all over with the sugar, leaving a 1 cm (½ inch) border on one of the shorter edges. Level the sugar with the back of a spoon so it is evenly spread.

Brush a little of the beaten egg on the uncovered border, then roll the pastry from the opposite edge and press lightly to seal.

Cut into 12 equal slices, each about 2 cm (¾ inch) thick. Arrange the slices in a 20 cm (8 inch) round cake tin so they are just touching, and brush with the remaining egg. Cook in a preheated air fryer at 190°C (375°F) for 15–16 minutes, until golden and risen and the base is crispy.

Meanwhile, mix the icing sugar with 1 teaspoon of the measured water, adding a little more water if necessary, until the icing is thick and just runs off the spoon. Transfer the rolls to a wire rack and drizzle over the icing. Serve warm.

MAKES 4
Preparation time 4 minutes
Cooking time 16 minutes

TOMATO & COURGETTE FRITTATAS

1 courgette, grated
4 eggs
1 tablespoon chopped chives
50 g (2 oz) ricotta cheese
2 teaspoons sunflower oil
8 cherry or baby plum tomatoes,
     halved
salt and pepper
chilli jam, to serve

Squeeze the grated courgette in a clean tea towel to remove excess water. Whisk together the eggs, chives and ricotta in a large jug and season well. Stir in the courgette.

Place ½ teaspoon of the oil in the bottom of each of 2 nonstick baking tins, about 10 cm (4 inches) in diameter. Place the tins in a preheated air fryer at 180°C (350°F) for 2 minutes to heat.

Divide half the egg mixture between the 2 tins and add 4 tomato halves to each. Cook for 7–8 minutes, until golden on top and cooked through. Repeat with the remaining ingredients.

Serve immediately with chilli jam.

SERVES 2
Preparation time 5 minutes
Cooking time 8 minutes

BRIOCHE CINNAMON FRENCH TOAST

1 large egg
½ teaspoon ground cinnamon
1 tablespoon caster sugar
50 ml (2 fl oz) milk
2 thick slices of brioche
sunflower oil, for spritzing
maple syrup, to serve

Whisk together the egg, cinnamon and sugar in a shallow bowl, then whisk in the milk. Add the slices of brioche, leave for a few minutes to soak up some of the mixture, then turn over and leave until all the egg mixture has been absorbed.

Place the bread in a preheated air fryer, spritz with a little oil and cook at 200°C (400°F) for 4 minutes. Turn over and cook for a further 3–4 minutes, until golden. Serve immediately, drizzled with maple syrup.

SERVES 2
Preparation time 5 minutes
Cooking time 9 minutes

TOMATO-STUFFED PORTOBELLO MUSHROOMS ON TOAST

100 g (3½ oz) baby spinach

2 tablespoons sundried tomato paste, plus extra for brushing

4 large Portobello mushrooms

16 cherry tomatoes

2 slices of wholemeal bread, toasted and halved

salt and pepper

handful of basil leaves, to garnish

Place the spinach in a colander and pour over boiling water to wilt. Allow to drain and when cool enough to handle, squeeze out the excess water. Place the spinach in a bowl and stir in the sundried tomato paste.

Hold the mushrooms by their stalks and brush the tops with a little sundried tomato paste. Cook the mushrooms, gill sides down, in a preheated air fryer at 200°C (400°F) for 5 minutes.

Turn the mushrooms over and divide the spinach mixture between them, then top each with 4 cherry tomatoes. Season well with salt and pepper and cook for a further 4 minutes, until tender.

Arrange 1 mushroom on each half slice of toast and garnish with the basil leaves before serving.

SERVES 4
Preparation time 5 minutes, plus cooling
Cooking time 15 minutes

BUCKWHEAT & TROPICAL FRUIT MUESLI

150 g (5 oz) buckwheat

50 g (2 oz) porridge oats

25 g (1 oz) chia seeds

2 tablespoons mixed seeds, such as pumpkin, sunflower and linseed

2 tablespoons melted coconut oil

1 teaspoon ground ginger

1 tablespoon agave or maple syrup

125 g (4 oz) dried mixed tropical fruit, such as pineapple, mango and papaya, chopped

50 g (2 oz) dried toasted coconut flakes or shavings

plant-based milk or yogurt, to serve

Mix all the ingredients, except the dried fruit and coconut, in a large bowl until well combined.

Spread the muesli over a piece of pierced nonstick baking paper in a preheated air fryer and cook at 150°C (300°F) for 13–15 minutes, until golden, stirring once.

Remove from the air fryer and allow to cool. Stir in the dried fruit and coconut and store in an airtight container for up to 4 weeks. Serve with plant-based milk or yogurt.

MAKES 4
Preparation time 10 minutes
Cooking time 15 minutes

BANANA & BLUEBERRY MUFFINS

1 banana, mashed

3 tablespoons sunflower or light olive oil

4 tablespoons plant-based milk

100 g (3½ oz) self-raising flour

25 g (1 oz) porridge oats

½ teaspoon ground cinnamon

1 teaspoon baking powder

½ teaspoon salt

2 tablespoons caster sugar

75 g (3 oz) blueberries

Line 4 small cake tins or ramekins with paper muffin cases. In a jug, whisk together the mashed banana, oil and milk.

Stir together the flour, oats, cinnamon, baking powder, salt and sugar in a large bowl, then stir the wet ingredients into the dry ingredients, until just combined. Stir in the blueberries.

Divide the mixture between the paper cases and level the tops. Place the tins in a preheated air fryer and cook at 160°C (325°F) for 14–15 minutes, until springy to the touch. Allow to cool for a few minutes, then transfer to a wire rack to cool completely. Store any leftover muffins in an airtight container for 1–2 days.

SERVES 2
Preparation time 10 minutes
Cooking time 6 minutes

CINNAMON-SUGAR TORTILLA CHIPS WITH FRUIT SALSA

1 tablespoon caster sugar
½ teaspoon ground cinnamon
2 flour tortillas
2 teaspoons vegan butter,
   melted
plant-based yogurt, to serve

Fresh fruit salsa
1 ripe mango, peeled, stoned
   and cut into small cubes
4 strawberries, hulled and cut
   into small pieces
1 kiwi, peeled and cut into small
   pieces
1 teaspoon grated fresh root
   ginger
1 tablespoon orange juice

Mix together the sugar and cinnamon in a small bowl. Brush the top of each tortilla with the melted butter, then sprinkle over the cinnamon sugar. Cut each tortilla into 8 wedges.

Cook the tortilla wedges in a preheated air fryer at 160°C (325°F) for 5–6 minutes, shaking halfway through, until golden. You may need to do this in 2 batches. Transfer to a wire rack – they will continue to crisp as they cool.

Meanwhile, mix all the salsa ingredients together in a bowl.

Serve the tortilla chips with the salsa, with a spoonful of plant-based yogurt on the side.

SERVES 2
Preparation time 10 minutes
Cooking time 8 minutes

CRUNCHY OAT BANANAS

2 small bananas, peeled
125 ml (4 fl oz) plant-based
   Greek-style yogurt, plus extra
   to serve
½ teaspoon ground mixed spice
50 g (2 oz) porridge oats
25 g (1 oz) pecans
2 tablespoons mixed seeds,
   such as pumpkin, sunflower
   and linseed
sunflower oil, for spritzing
date or maple syrup, to serve

Cut the bananas in half lengthways, then cut each piece in half so you have 8 pieces in total. Place the yogurt and mixed spice in a bowl and stir well.

Place the oats and nuts in a small food processor and blitz to a coarse crumb. Tip on to a plate and stir in the seeds. Dunk each banana piece in the yogurt mixture to fully coat, then roll in the oat mixture.

Spritz generously with oil, then cook in a preheated air fryer at 200°C (400°F) for 6–8 minutes, turning once, until golden and crispy. Serve warm with extra yogurt and date or maple syrup to drizzle.

SERVES 2
Preparation time 5 minutes, plus marinating
Cooking time 10 minutes

KING OYSTER MUSHROOM, LETTUCE & TOMATO SANDWICHES

2 tablespoons kecap manis

1 teaspoon smoked paprika

1 tablespoon maple syrup

1 teaspoon sunflower oil

1 teaspoon cider or white wine vinegar

2 large king oyster mushrooms, sliced

4 slices of wholemeal bread

2 tablespoons vegan mayonnaise

6 Little Gem lettuce leaves

1 tomato, sliced

salt and pepper

Place the kecap manis, smoked paprika, maple syrup, oil, vinegar and salt and pepper in a shallow bowl and stir well. Add the mushrooms, turn in the sauce, then cover and leave to marinate for 10 minutes at room temperature.

Cook the mushrooms in a single layer in preheated air fryer at 200°C (400°F) for 8–10 minutes, turning once and brushing with any remaining marinade, until starting to crisp.

Meanwhile, spread 2 slices of the bread with the mayonnaise and top with the lettuce leaves and sliced tomato. Top with the mushrooms and the other slices of bread, cut in half and serve immediately.

MAKES 12
Preparation time 15 minutes
Cooking time 20 minutes

BUCKWHEAT & BANANA PANCAKES

75 g (3 oz) buckwheat flour
1 teaspoon baking powder
pinch of salt
1 banana, sliced, plus extra to
serve
150 ml (¼ pint) plant-based milk
1 tablespoon sunflower oil, plus
extra for greasing
1 tablespoon maple syrup, plus
extra to serve
plant-based yogurt, to serve

Place the flour and baking powder in a mixing bowl with a pinch of salt and stir well. In a jug, mash the banana with a fork, then beat in the milk, oil and maple syrup. Gradually pour the wet ingredients into the flour mixture and whisk until you have a smooth batter.

Grease the base and sides of each of 3 nonstick baking tins, about 10 cm (4 inches) in diameter. Place the tins in a preheated air fryer at 200°C (400°F) for 2 minutes to heat.

Spoon a heaped tablespoon of the batter into each tin to cover the base, place the tins in the air fryer and cook for 6–7 minutes, until golden. Keep warm while you cook the remaining pancakes.

Serve the pancakes drizzled with maple syrup, with a dollop of plant-based yogurt and some sliced bananas on the side.

SERVES 2
Preparation time 4 minutes
Cooking time 13 minutes

SPICED TOFU SCRAMBLE

200 g (7 oz) firm smoked tofu

1 small red onion, thinly sliced

1 teaspoon sunflower oil

2 teaspoons mild or medium
   curry powder

2 tomatoes, chopped

50 g (2 oz) baby spinach,
   roughly chopped

salt and pepper

To serve
vegan chapatis
mango chutney

Dry the tofu on kitchen paper and cut into bite-sized pieces.

Place the onion in an ovenproof dish and drizzle over the oil. Place the dish in a preheated air fryer at 190°C (375°F) and cook for 2 minutes, until softened. Stir in the curry powder and cook for 1 minute.

Mix in the tomatoes and tofu and cook for 5 minutes, until the tofu is starting to turn golden, then gently stir. Cook for a further 4 minutes, until the tofu is golden on all sides.

Stir in the spinach and cook for 1 minute, until just wilted. Season with salt and pepper, divide between 2 plates and serve immediately with vegan chapatis and mango chutney.

EASY
SPEEDY
MAINS

SERVES 2
Preparation time 5 minutes
Cooking time 12 minutes

BAKED FETA & TOMATO PASTA

225 g (7½ oz) cherry tomatoes
1 garlic clove, chopped
100 g (3½ oz) piece of
    vegetarian feta cheese
1 tablespoon olive oil
pinch of dried chilli flakes
200 g (7 oz) dried penne pasta
2 tablespoons sliced black
    olives (optional)
salt and pepper
1 tablespoon basil leaves,
    to garnish

Arrange the tomatoes and garlic in an ovenproof dish and nestle the feta in the middle. Drizzle over the olive oil, sprinkle over the chilli flakes and season with pepper.

Place the dish in a preheated air fryer and cook at 190°C (375°F) for 10 minutes, gently shaking the tomatoes halfway through, until the feta is soft and the tomatoes have burst.

Meanwhile, cook the pasta in a saucepan of lightly salted boiling water according to the packet instructions, until just tender. Drain, reserving 2 tablespoons of the cooking water.

Stir the drained pasta into the tomatoes and feta, with the olives, if using, adding 1–2 tablespoons of the reserved water to make a creamy sauce. Divide between 2 bowls and serve immediately, sprinkled with pepper and the basil leaves.

SERVES 3–4
Preparation time 15 minutes, plus marinating
Cooking time 40 minutes

WHOLE ROASTED CAULIFLOWER

1 small cauliflower
½ teaspoon ground turmeric
½ teaspoon salt

Marinade
100 ml (3½ fl oz) coconut yogurt
2 teaspoons grated fresh root
    ginger
1 garlic clove, crushed
2 tablespoons tandoori spice
    mix
1 tablespoon sunflower oil
1 tablespoon lemon juice
½ teaspoon salt

To serve
3–4 mini naan breads, warmed
½ red onion, thinly sliced
ready-made cucumber raita
2 tablespoons chopped fresh
    coriander

Trim the leaves off the cauliflower and trim the stalk so that it sits flat. Cut a cross in the stalk. Bring a large saucepan of water to the boil and add the turmeric and salt. Gently lower in the cauliflower and simmer for 4 minutes, turning halfway through. Drain in a colander and leave to steam dry, stalk side up.

Meanwhile, mix together all the marinade ingredients in a large bowl. Add the cauliflower and coat all over on both sides. Leave to marinate for at least 30 minutes, or overnight.

Cook the cauliflower, florets side up, in a preheated air fryer at 160°C (325°F) for 30–35 minutes, until tender, then cut into pieces. Serve on the warmed naans with the red onion, raita and fresh coriander.

SERVES 2
Preparation time 5 minutes
Cooking time 20 minutes

ROASTED BALSAMIC VEGETABLES & HALLOUMI

1 red or yellow pepper, cored, deseeded and cut into chunks
1 courgette, thickly sliced
1 red onion, cut into 8 wedges
2 garlic cloves, peeled
2 teaspoons olive oil
2 teaspoons balsamic vinegar
1 teaspoon Italian dried mixed herbs
8 baby plum or cherry tomatoes
125 g (4 oz) vegetarian halloumi cheese, cut into 6 slices
salt and pepper
ciabatta bread, to serve

Place the red or yellow pepper, courgette and onion wedges in a bowl, add the garlic, oil, vinegar and dried herbs and season well, then toss to coat. Cook in a preheated air fryer at 180°C (350°F) for 12 minutes.

Gently stir the vegetables, then add the tomatoes and arrange the halloumi slices on top. Cook for a further 6–8 minutes, until the tomatoes have softened and the cheese is golden.

Divide between 2 plates, drizzle with any juices from the bottom of the air fryer and serve with warm ciabatta bread.

SERVES 2
Preparation time 15 minutes
Cooking time 28 minutes

AUBERGINE 'PARMIGIANA'

2 small aubergines, cut lengthways into 5 mm (¼ inch) slices
2 tablespoons olive oil
1 teaspoon salt
150 g (5 oz) vegetarian mozzarella, drained and sliced
8 basil leaves
25 g (1 oz) vegetarian Italian-style hard cheese, grated
crisp green salad, to serve

Tomato sauce
1 tablespoon olive oil
1 small onion, chopped
1 garlic clove, crushed
400 g (13 oz) can chopped tomatoes
1 teaspoon balsamic vinegar
1 teaspoon dried oregano
salt and pepper

Brush the aubergine slices on both sides with the olive oil and sprinkle with the salt. Cook half the aubergine slices in a single layer in a preheated air fryer at 200°C (400°F) for 4 minutes, then turn over and cook for a further 4 minutes, until softened. Layer the cooked slices in the bottom of an ovenproof dish. Cook the remaining aubergine in the same way, then set aside.

Meanwhile, make the sauce. Heat the oil in a saucepan over a medium heat, add the onion and garlic and cook for 3–4 minutes, until softened. Stir in the tomatoes, vinegar and oregano and bring to the boil, then reduce the heat and simmer for 12–14 minutes, until reduced and thickened slightly. Season to taste.

Spread the sauce over the aubergines in the ovenproof dish. Add the mozzarella and basil leaves, then top with the reserved aubergine slices. Sprinkle over the Italian-style hard cheese.

Place the dish in the air fryer and cook at 180°C (350°F) for 10 minutes, until the top is golden, the sauce is bubbling and the cheese has melted. Serve with a crisp green salad.

SERVES 2
Preparation time 15 minutes
Cooking time 27 minutes

CREAMY MUSTARD VEGETABLE PIE

1 leek, trimmed, cleaned and cut
    into 1 cm (½ inch) slices
1 potato, peeled and cut into
    1.5 cm (¾ inch) pieces
2 carrots, peeled and cut into
    1.5 cm (¾ inch) pieces
2 teaspoons olive oil
leaves from 1 thyme sprig
4 teaspoons vegetable gravy
    granules
300 ml (½ pint) boiling water
2 teaspoons wholegrain
    mustard
2 tablespoons crème fraîche
milk or beaten egg, to glaze
salt and pepper
green beans, to serve

Suet pastry
100 g (3½ oz) self-raising flour,
    plus extra for dusting
50 g (2 oz) vegetable suet
½ teaspoon salt
25 g (1 oz) mature vegetarian
    Cheddar cheese, grated
100 ml (3½ fl oz) cold water

Place the leek, potato and carrots in a bowl, drizzle over the oil, add the thyme and season well. Toss to coat. Cook the vegetables in a preheated air fryer at 180°C (350°F) for 12–15 minutes, shaking the basket halfway through, until tender.

Meanwhile, make the pastry. Place the flour, suet, salt and cheese in a bowl, then stir in the measured cold water to make a soft, slightly sticky dough. Leave to rest for 5 minutes.

Transfer the vegetables to a bowl. Place the gravy granules in a measuring jug, pour over the boiling water and stir until thickened, then stir in the mustard. Pour the mixture over the vegetables, add the crème fraîche, then stir well. Divide between 2 pie dishes, about 12 cm (5 inches) in length, or 1 large ovenproof dish.

Roll out the pastry on a lightly floured surface and cut out 2 strips to fit around the edges of the pie dishes, plus 2 discs for the pie tops, making them slightly larger than the dishes. Brush the outside edges of the dishes with a little water and stick the strips around the tops. Brush the pastry strips with a little more water and stick the pastry tops in place. Press to seal and trim off any excess.

Brush the pastry with a little milk or beaten egg and make a slit in the centre of each pie for the steam to escape. Cook the pies in the air fryer for 10–12 minutes, until the pastry is golden and the filling bubbling. Serve with green beans.

SERVES 2
Preparation time 10 minutes
Cooking time 22 minutes

ROASTED TOMATOES & PEPPERS WITH BURRATA & GARLIC TOASTS

25 g (1 oz) basil leaves, plus
    extra to garnish
finely grated zest and juice of
    ½ lemon
1½ tablespoons extra virgin
    olive oil
1 tablespoon pine nuts
4 slices of ciabatta bread
1 garlic clove, peeled
2 x 150 g (5 oz) vegetarian
    burrata, drained
salt and pepper

Roasted tomatoes & peppers
1 garlic clove, sliced
250 g (8 oz) red and yellow
    cherry tomatoes
1 red pepper, cored, deseeded
    and cut into thick strips
1 yellow pepper, cored,
    deseeded and cut into thick
    strips
1 teaspoon extra virgin olive oil
2 teaspoons balsamic vinegar

For the roasted tomatoes and peppers, place the garlic in a bowl with the cherry tomatoes and peppers, drizzle with the olive oil and season with salt and pepper. Cook in a preheated air fryer at 160°C (325°F) for 15–20 minutes, gently shaking the basket halfway through, until softened and slightly charred. Return to the bowl, drizzle over the balsamic vinegar and leave to cool.

Meanwhile, place the basil, lemon zest and juice, olive oil and a pinch of salt in a small food processor and blitz to make a dressing.

Place the pine nuts in a dry frying pan over a medium heat, stirring occasionally, until lightly toasted.

Toast the ciabatta slices in the air fryer at 200°C (400°F) for 1 minute on each side, until lightly golden. Rub with the peeled garlic clove.

Divide the roasted tomatoes and peppers between 2 plates, top each plate with a burrata, then scatter with the pine nuts. Drizzle over the basil dressing and garnish with a few basil leaves. Serve with a good grind of black pepper and the garlic toasts.

SERVES 4
Preparation time 5 minutes
Cooking time 45 minutes

LOADED SWEET POTATOES WITH LENTILS, CARAMELIZED ONION & CHEESE

4 sweet potatoes, scrubbed

2 tablespoons olive oil

2 teaspoons sea salt

1 teaspoon freshly ground black pepper

250 g (8 oz) pouch ready-cooked Puy lentils

4 tablespoons caramelized onion chutney

75 g (3 oz) mature vegetarian Cheddar cheese, grated

50 g (2 oz) walnuts, chopped

75 g (3 oz) rocket leaves

Prick the sweet potatoes all over with a fork, rub with half the oil and sprinkle with the salt and pepper. Cook slightly apart in a preheated air fryer at 190°C (375°F) for 35–40 minutes, turning halfway through, until tender.

Towards the end of the cooking time, warm the lentils with a dash of water in a saucepan over a low heat until piping hot, then stir in the remaining oil and the onion chutney.

Cut the sweet potatoes in half and fluff up the flesh with a fork. Divide the lentil mixture between them and sprinkle with the grated cheese. Return 4 halves to the air fryer and cook for 2–3 minutes, until the cheese has melted. Repeat with the remaining sweet potato halves. Meanwhile, place the walnuts in a dry frying pan over a medium heat, stirring occasionally, until lightly toasted.

Arrange 2 sweet potato halves on each plate. Top with the walnuts and a large handful of rocket leaves and serve immediately.

SERVES 2
Preparation time 8 minutes
Cooking time 12 minutes

SWEET & SOUR CHILLI PANEER

225 g (7½ oz) paneer, cut into
    1.5 cm (¾ inch) cubes
1 tablespoon cornflour
½ teaspoon hot chilli powder
½ teaspoon salt
1 teaspoon sunflower oil, plus
    extra for spritzing
1 red pepper, cored, deseeded
    and chopped
4 spring onions, cut into 1.5 cm
    (¾ inch) pieces, plus extra,
    thinly sliced, to garnish
2 canned pineapple rings in
    juice, drained and chopped
medium egg noodles, to serve

Sweet & sour sauce
1 tablespoon tomato ketchup
1 tablespoon tomato purée
1 tablespoon light soy sauce
2 tablespoons rice wine vinegar
3 tablespoons pineapple juice
    from the can
1 teaspoon grated fresh root
    ginger

Place the paneer in a bowl, add the cornflour, chilli powder and salt and toss gently to coat.

Pour the oil into a baking tin, then place the tin in a preheated air fryer at 190°C (375°F) for 1 minute to heat. Add the paneer, red pepper and spring onions, spritz with a little oil and cook for 10 minutes, stirring gently halfway through, until tender.

Meanwhile, mix together all the sauce ingredients. Stir the pineapple pieces into the paneer mixture and pour over the sauce. Stir gently to coat, then cook for 2 minutes, until the sauce is bubbling. Serve immediately with noodles, garnished with sliced spring onions.

SERVES 4
Preparation time 15 minutes
Cooking time 27 minutes

CHEESE & ONION PASTIES

1 potato (about 225 g/7½ oz), peeled and cut into 1 cm (½ inch) dice

1 onion, cut into 1 cm (½ inch) dice

1 teaspoon dried mixed herbs

2 teaspoons sunflower or light olive oil

½ teaspoon salt

325 g (11 oz) ready-made shortcrust pastry

flour, for dusting

2 tablespoons double cream

100 g (3½ oz) mature vegetarian Cheddar cheese, grated

1 egg, beaten

freshly ground black pepper

baked beans, to serve

Place the potato, onion, dried herbs, oil and salt in a bowl with a good grinding of black pepper and mix well.

Cook in a preheated air fryer at 180°C (350°F) for 10–12 minutes, shaking the basket halfway through, until just tender. Transfer to a bowl to cool.

Meanwhile, divide the pastry into 4 pieces and roll each out on a lightly floured surface to about 4 mm (just under ¼ inch) thick. Cut a 15 cm (6 inch) disc from each piece.

Stir the cream and cheese into the cooled vegetable mixture. Pile a quarter of the filling on one side of each pastry disc, leaving a 2.5 cm (1 inch) border around the edge. Brush the edges of the pastry with a little beaten egg, then fold the bare pastry over the filling and press around the edges to enclose it. Stand the pasties upright, crimp the edges of the pastry to seal, then brush all over with beaten egg.

Cook the pasties on a piece of pierced nonstick baking paper in a preheated air fryer at 180°C (350°F) for 12 minutes, until golden. Turn the pasties over and cook for a further 3 minutes to allow the bases to crisp. Serve with baked beans.

SERVES 2
Preparation time 12 minutes
Cooking time 15 minutes

CHICKPEA FAJITAS

400 g (13 oz) can chickpeas,
    drained and rinsed
1 red pepper, cored, deseeded
    and sliced
1 yellow pepper, cored,
    deseeded and sliced
1 garlic clove, crushed
finely grated zest and juice of
    1 lime
2 teaspoons sunflower oil
2 tablespoons fajita spice mix

Salsa
2 tomatoes, deseeded and diced
1 red onion, thinly sliced
finely grated zest and juice of
    1 lime
salt

To serve
4 flour or corn tortillas
soured cream
grated vegetarian Cheddar
    cheese
chopped fresh coriander
lime wedges

Place the chickpeas, peppers and garlic in a large bowl with the lime zest and juice. Drizzle over the oil and add the spice mix, then stir to coat. Cook in a preheated air fryer at 180°C (350°F) for 12–15 minutes, stirring once, until the chickpeas are crispy and the peppers lightly charred.

Meanwhile, place all the salsa ingredients in a bowl and stir well.

To serve, warm the tortillas according to the packet instructions, spoon over some of the chickpea and pepper mixture and top with the salsa, soured cream and grated cheese. Sprinkle with a little fresh coriander, squeeze over a little lime juice, then roll up and enjoy.

SERVES 4
Preparation time 10 minutes
Cooking time 30 minutes

ROASTED BEETROOT, BUTTER BEAN & HERBY GOATS' CHEESE SALAD

8 raw beetroot, trimmed, scrubbed and quartered

1 teaspoon olive oil

1 teaspoon balsamic vinegar

1 red pepper, cored, deseeded and cut into 2.5 cm (1 inch) pieces

2 x 400 g (13 oz) cans butter beans, drained and rinsed

150 g (5 oz) soft vegetarian goats' cheese

1 tablespoon chopped chives

3 tarragon sprigs, leaves picked and finely chopped

150 g (5 oz) mixed baby spinach, watercress and rocket leaves

50 g (2 oz) walnuts

salt and pepper

Dressing

1 teaspoon Dijon mustard

1 tablespoon lemon juice

2 tablespoons olive oil

Place the beetroot in a bowl, drizzle over the oil and vinegar and season well with salt and pepper. Cook in a preheated air fryer at 190°C (375°F) for 20 minutes, then turn the beetroot and add the red pepper. Cook for a further 10 minutes, until the beetroot and red pepper are tender. Allow to cool slightly, then stir in the beans.

Meanwhile, beat the goats' cheese together with the herbs.

Whisk the dressing ingredients together and season to taste. Pour over the salad leaves and gently toss together.

Place the walnuts in a dry frying pan over a medium heat, stirring occasionally, until lightly toasted.

Divide the salad leaves between 4 plates and arrange the beetroot and bean mixture over the top. Dot with spoonfuls of the goats' cheese, scatter over the walnuts and serve immediately.

SERVES 2
Preparation time 10 minutes
Cooking time 30 minutes

STUFFED TOMATOES WITH RICE & PESTO

4 beefsteak tomatoes
1 tablespoon olive oil
1 onion, finely chopped
1 garlic clove, crushed
250 g (8 oz) pouch ready-cooked
    wild and white rice
4 sundried tomatoes, chopped
4 tablespoons fresh vegetarian
    basil pesto
25 g (1 oz) vegetarian Italian-
    style hard cheese, grated
finely grated zest of ½ lemon
salt and pepper
rocket salad, to serve

Cut a 1.5 cm (¾ inch) thick slice off the top of each tomato and reserve. Using a melon baller or teaspoon, scoop the pulp out of the tomatoes into a bowl and set aside.

Heat the oil in a saucepan over a medium heat, add the onion and garlic and cook for 2–3 minutes, until softened but not browned. Add the tomato pulp, increase the heat slightly and simmer for 7–8 minutes, stirring occasionally, until the mixture is reduced and thickened.

Stir in the rice, sundried tomatoes and pesto and cook for 2–3 minutes to heat through. Stir in most of the cheese and the lemon zest and season to taste.

Place the tomatoes in an ovenproof dish and fill with the rice mixture. Sprinkle with the remaining cheese and replace the tops. Place the dish in a preheated air fryer at 160°C (325°F) and cook for 15 minutes, until the tomatoes are tender. Serve 2 tomatoes per person with a rocket salad on the side.

SERVES 2
Preparation time 5 minutes
Cooking time 22 minutes

CRISPY GNOCCHI WITH BUTTERNUT SQUASH & SPINACH

250 g (8 oz) butternut squash, peeled, deseeded and cut into 2.5 cm (1 inch) cubes
1 tablespoon olive oil
250 g (8 oz) vegan gnocchi
1 small red onion, cut into wedges
8 sage leaves
50 g (2 oz) baby spinach
2 tablespoons vegan basil pesto
1 tablespoon pine nuts
salt and pepper

Place the butternut squash in a bowl and add 1 teaspoon of the oil. Toss with a little salt and pepper. Cook in a preheated air fryer at 200°C (400°F) for 10 minutes, shaking the basket halfway through.

Toss the gnocchi, onion wedges and sage leaves in the remaining oil, add to the air fryer and cook for a further 10–12 minutes, shaking the basket a couple of times, until the gnocchi is crispy and the squash is tender. Add the spinach about 1 minute before the end of the cooking time. Stir well so the spinach is all wilted.

Meanwhile, place the pine nuts in a dry frying pan over a medium heat, stirring occasionally, until lightly toasted.

Transfer to a serving plate, drizzle with the pesto and sprinkle with a good grind of black pepper and the pine nuts. Serve immediately.

SERVES 2
Preparation time 20 minutes
Cooking time 25 minutes

KATSU SWEET POTATO CURRY

1 large sweet potato, peeled
4 tablespoons plain flour
4 tablespoons cold water
50 g (2 oz) panko breadcrumbs
olive oil, for spritzing
salt and pepper

Katsu sauce
1 tablespoon sunflower oil
1 onion, finely chopped
2 garlic cloves, crushed
2.5 cm (1 inch) piece of fresh
    root ginger, peeled and finely
    grated
1 carrot, diced
1 tablespoon mild curry powder
1 teaspoon ground turmeric
1 tablespoon plain flour
300 ml (½ pint) vegan vegetable
    stock
100 ml (3½ fl oz) coconut milk
1 teaspoon soy sauce
2 teaspoons apple sauce

To serve
steamed rice
salad leaves

Heat the oil for the sauce in a saucepan over a medium heat, add the onion, garlic and ginger and cook for 2 minutes, then stir in the carrot. Cover and cook over a low heat for 10 minutes, stirring occasionally, until the vegetables have softened and are starting to caramelize.

Stir in the spices and flour and cook for 2 minutes, then gradually stir in the stock. Add the coconut milk, soy and apple sauce, reduce the heat and simmer, uncovered, for 10 minutes. Season to taste, then press the sauce through a sieve.

Meanwhile, cut the sweet potato on the diagonal into 8 slices, about 1 cm (½ inch) thick.

Place the flour in a small bowl and stir in the measured water to make a smooth paste, then season with a little salt and pepper. Place the breadcrumbs on a plate. Dip each slice of sweet potato in the paste to coat and then in the breadcrumbs.

Arrange the sweet potato slices in a single layer in a preheated air fryer, spritz with a little oil and cook at 180°C (350°F) for 18–20 minutes, turning halfway through and spritzing with a little more oil, until the sweet potato is tender and crisp on the outside. Serve the sweet potato slices with the curry sauce, some steamed rice and salad leaves.

SERVES 4
Preparation time 15 minutes
Cooking time 12 minutes

BARBECUE MUSHROOM BURGERS WITH KIMCHI SLAW

4 tablespoons sesame seeds
4 large Portobello mushrooms
crisp green lettuce leaves
4 vegan burger buns, halved
    and toasted

Korean barbecue sauce
1 teaspoon toasted sesame oil
2 tablespoons rice wine vinegar
1 tablespoon light soft brown
    sugar
1 tablespoon dark soy sauce
1 garlic clove, crushed
1 teaspoon grated fresh root
    ginger
1 tablespoon gochujang

Kimchi slaw
4 tablespoons vegan
    mayonnaise
4 tablespoons vegan kimchi,
    roughly chopped
4 spring onions, chopped
1 small carrot, coarsely grated

Place all the sauce ingredients in a small saucepan over a medium heat and cook, stirring, until all the ingredients are combined, then simmer for 3 minutes, until glossy and slightly thickened. Set aside.

Combine all the slaw ingredients in a bowl and mix well.

Place the sesame seeds on a plate. Hold each mushroom by the stalk and brush it all over with the sauce, then dip in the seeds to lightly coat.

Arrange the mushrooms, gill sides down, in a preheated air fryer and cook at 200°C (400°F) for 5 minutes, then turn over and cook for a further 4 minutes, until tender.

Pile some lettuce leaves on the base of each bun and top with a mushroom and a generous amount of the slaw. Top with the lids and serve immediately.

SERVES 2
Preparation time 5 minutes
Cooking time 24 minutes

MISO-GLAZED AUBERGINES

2 small aubergines
2 tablespoons sunflower oil
4 tablespoons white miso paste
2 tablespoons rice wine vinegar
  or mirin
2 tablespoons sake or water
1 tablespoon caster sugar
1 tablespoon black and white
  sesame seeds
2 spring onions, thinly sliced
steamed jasmine rice, to serve

Cut the aubergines in half lengthways, then score the cut sides of the flesh in a diamond pattern, being careful not to cut all the way through. Brush the flesh of each aubergine with the oil, then cook, cut side up, in a preheated air fryer at 190°C (375°F) for 12 minutes, until softened.

Mix together the miso paste, rice wine vinegar, sake and sugar in a small bowl. Brush the aubergines with half the miso glaze and cook for a further 12 minutes, brushing with the remaining glaze halfway through, until softened, sticky and caramelized.

Meanwhile, place the sesame seeds in a dry frying pan over a medium heat, stirring occasionally, until lightly toasted.

Sprinkle with the sesame seeds and spring onions and serve with steamed jasmine rice.

SERVES 4
Preparation time 10 minutes
Cooking time 26 minutes

VEGETABLE & CHICKPEA TAGINE

2 parsnips, cut into 2.5 cm (1 inch) chunks

2 carrots, cut into 2.5 cm (1 inch) chunks

1 red onion, cut into 8 wedges

2 teaspoons olive oil

2 teaspoons Moroccan spice mix

4 tomatoes, quartered

300 ml (½ pint) hot vegan vegetable stock

2 teaspoons harissa paste

1 tablespoon tomato purée

400 g (13 oz) can chickpeas, drained and rinsed

50 g (2 oz) pitted green olives

6 dried apricots, chopped

1 preserved lemon, halved, flesh discarded and skin chopped

salt and pepper

2 tablespoons chopped flat leaf parsley, to garnish

couscous, to serve

Place the parsnips, carrots and onions in a bowl, drizzle over the oil and sprinkle over the spice mix. Season and toss well to coat.

Cook in a preheated air fryer at 180°C (350°F) for 14 minutes, shaking the basket halfway through and adding the tomatoes.

Remove any crisping plates or baskets from the air fryer, then tip the vegetables into the base and add all the remaining ingredients. Cook for a further 12 minutes, stirring halfway through. Season to taste, sprinkle with the parsley and serve with couscous.

SERVES 2–3
Preparation time 15 minutes
Cooking time 10 minutes

PULLED OYSTER MUSHROOM TACOS WITH PINEAPPLE SALSA

250 g (8 oz) king oyster
  mushrooms
2 teaspoons sunflower oil
1 onion, chopped
1 garlic clove, crushed
1 teaspoon ground cumin
1 teaspoon smoked paprika
1 tablespoon ancho or chipotle
  chilli paste
2 tablespoons dark soy sauce
1 tablespoon maple syrup
1 tablespoon tomato ketchup

Pineapple salsa
175 g (6 oz) fresh pineapple, cut
  into 1 cm (½ inch) dice
grated zest and juice of 1 lime
1 small red chilli, deseeded and
  finely chopped
2 tablespoons chopped fresh
  coriander

To serve
4–6 small flour tortillas
ready-made guacamole
shredded lettuce

Prepare the mushrooms by cutting off the caps and slicing them into thin strips. Shred the stems by scoring down the length with a fork, turning to shred all sides, then tear the shredded stems into long pieces using your hands. Set aside.

Place the oil in an ovenproof dish, add the onion, garlic, cumin and smoked paprika and stir together. Place the dish in a preheated air fryer at 180°C (350°F) and cook for 2 minutes, stirring halfway through.

Meanwhile, mix the chilli paste, soy sauce, maple syrup and tomato ketchup in a large bowl and stir in the mushrooms to coat. Stir into the dish with the onion and cook for 8 minutes, stirring halfway through.

Meanwhile, make the salsa by mixing together all the ingredients in a serving bowl. Chill in the refrigerator until ready to use.

To serve, warm the tortillas according to the packet instructions. Place the guacamole, lettuce and mushrooms in separate bowls and build your own tacos, topping with a spoonful of the salsa.

SERVES 4
Preparation time 15 minutes, plus pressing
    and marinating
Cooking time 12 minutes

TERIYAKI TOFU & VEGETABLE KEBABS

400 g (13 oz) firm tofu
1 red pepper, cored, deseeded
    and cut into cubes
4 spring onions, cut into 2.5 cm
    (1 inch) pieces, plus extra,
    thinly sliced, to garnish
1 tablespoon sesame seeds
steamed rice, to serve

Marinade
2 tablespoons dark soy sauce
1 tablespoon mirin or rice wine
    vinegar
1 tablespoon light soft brown
    sugar
1 garlic clove, crushed
2 teaspoons finely grated fresh
    root ginger

Place the tofu between 2 pieces of kitchen paper and place a chopping board or other heavy weight on top. Leave for at least 15 minutes to remove excess water, then cut into 20 cubes, about 2.5 cm (1 inch) across.

Mix all the marinade ingredients in a large bowl and stir until the sugar has dissolved. Stir in the tofu and leave to marinate for at least 1 hour, or overnight.

Thread the tofu pieces and vegetables alternately on to 8 small metal skewers, or 8 wooden skewers that have been soaked in water to prevent them burning.

Cook in a single layer in a preheated air fryer at 180°C (350°F) for 10–12 minutes, turning once and brushing generously all over with the remaining marinade halfway through.

Meanwhile, place the sesame seeds in a dry frying pan over a medium heat, stirring occasionally, until lightly toasted.

Serve 2 kebabs per person, sprinkled with the toasted sesame seeds, with steamed rice, garnished with sliced spring onions.

SERVES 4
Preparation time 15 minutes
Cooking time 35 minutes

LENTIL & MUSHROOM MEATLESS BALLS

250 g (8 oz) chestnut
  mushrooms, roughly chopped
1 garlic clove, crushed
1 small onion, roughly chopped
1 tablespoon olive oil
250 g (8 oz) cooked green lentils
  from a pouch or can, drained
1 tablespoon tomato purée
2 tablespoons chopped flat leaf
  parsley
2 teaspoons dried mixed herbs
2 tablespoons dried
  breadcrumbs
25 g (1 oz) vegan Italian-style
  hard cheese, grated, plus
  extra to serve
350 g (11½ oz) dried spaghetti
salt and pepper
basil leaves, to garnish

Tomato sauce
1 tablespoon olive oil
1 onion, sliced
1 garlic clove, crushed
400 g (13 oz) can chopped
  tomatoes
400 ml (14 fl oz) passata
  (sieved tomatoes)
200 ml (7 fl oz) hot vegan
  vegetable stock
1 teaspoon dried oregano
1 teaspoon sugar
1 teaspoon salt

Place the mushrooms, garlic and onions in a bowl, pour over the oil, season to taste and toss well. Cook in a preheated air fryer at 180°C (350°F) for 10 minutes, shaking the basket halfway through, until softened. Cool slightly, then place in a food processor and pulse until finely chopped. Add the lentils, tomato purée, parsley, dried herbs, breadcrumbs and grated cheese and pulse until the mixture starts to come together. Shape the mixture into 16 balls and chill in the refrigerator while you make the sauce.

Heat the oil in a saucepan over a medium heat, add the onion and garlic and cook for 4–5 minutes, until softened but not browned. Stir in the remaining ingredients, season with pepper, then reduce the heat and simmer, uncovered, for 15 minutes, stirring occasionally.

Cook the meatballs in a preheated air fryer at 180°C (350°F) for 10 minutes towards the end of the sauce cooking time. Transfer to an ovenproof dish and pour over the tomato sauce. Place the dish in the air fryer and cook for 5 minutes. While the meatballs are cooking, cook the pasta in a saucepan of lightly salted boiling water according to the packet instructions, until just tender. Drain well.

Divide the pasta between 4 bowls, spoon over the meatballs and sauce, sprinkle over some cheese and garnish with basil leaves.

SERVES 2
Preparation time 10 minutes
Cooking time 18 minutes

CRISPY NORI TOFU & CHIPS

200 g (7 oz) firm tofu, cut into
    4 fingers about 2.5 cm (1 inch)
    thick
2 sheets of nori, halved
50 g (2 oz) panko breadcrumbs
250 g (8 oz) frozen oven chips
sunflower oil, for spritzing
salt and pepper

Batter
4 tablespoons plain flour
1 tablespoon lemon juice
3 tablespoons cold water

To serve
mushy peas
lemon wedges

Make the batter by placing the flour in a bowl and whisking in the lemon juice and measured water to make a thick consistency.

Season the tofu with salt and pepper and wrap each finger in a piece of nori, dampening the edges with a little water to seal – the moisture in the tofu will help it stick. Dip each finger in the batter to fully coat, then in the breadcrumbs.

Cook the chips in a preheated air fryer at 180°C (350°F) for 5 minutes. Shake the basket, then add the tofu, spritz with oil and cook for a further 10 minutes, turning the tofu and shaking the chips halfway through.

Remove the tofu from the air fryer when crispy, increase the temperature to 200°C (400°F) and cook the chips for a further 2–3 minutes, until crispy. Serve the tofu and chips with mushy peas and lemon wedges.

SERVES 2
Preparation time 10 minutes
Cooking time 34 minutes

CAPONATA

2 aubergines, cut into 2.5 cm
  (1 inch) pieces
1 tablespoon olive oil
1 large red onion, sliced
1 celery stick, cut into 1.5 cm
  (¾ inch) pieces
200 g (7 oz) ripe tomatoes,
  quartered
2 tablespoons pine nuts
200 ml (7 fl oz) passata
  (sieved tomatoes)
2 tablespoons red wine vinegar
1 tablespoon caster sugar
2 tablespoons pitted green
  olives, chopped
1 tablespoon capers, rinsed
2 tablespoons sultanas or
  raisins
small bunch of basil, shredded
salt and pepper
toasted ciabatta or pasta,
  to serve

Place the aubergines in a bowl and drizzle over the oil, season with a little salt and pepper, then toss to coat. Cook half the aubergines in a preheated air fryer at 190°C (375°F) for 9–10 minutes, shaking the basket once, until tender. Tip into a bowl, then repeat with the remaining aubergines.

Toss the onion, celery and tomatoes with the aubergines, then return to the air fryer and cook for 7 minutes.

Meanwhile, place the pine nuts in a dry frying pan over a medium heat, stirring occasionally, until lightly toasted.

Remove any crisping plates or baskets from the air fryer and tip the vegetables into the base. Add all the remaining ingredients, except the pine nuts and basil, stir well and cook for 5–7 minutes, stirring halfway through, until bubbling. Season with a little salt and pepper.

Allow to cool slightly, then stir in the pine nuts. Stir in the basil just before serving warm with toasted ciabatta.

SERVES 2
Preparation time 10 minutes
Cooking time 18 minutes

ROASTED CABBAGE WEDGES WITH CORIANDER & LEMON SAUCE

....

½ Savoy or green cabbage
1 tablespoon olive oil
1 tablespoon shawarma spice
   mix
½ teaspoon salt
½ teaspoon freshly ground
   black pepper

Coriander & lemon sauce
1 ripe avocado, halved and
   stoned
25 g (1 oz) fresh coriander,
   roughly chopped
finely grated zest and juice of
   1 lemon
1 tablespoon tahini
4 tablespoons water

To serve
brown rice
lemon wedges

Cut the cabbage into 4 wedges, keeping the core intact so the leaves stay together. Mix the oil, spice mix and salt and pepper in a bowl, then brush over both sides of the cabbage wedges. Cook in a preheated air fryer at 180°C (350°F) for 15–18 minutes, turning halfway through, until the outer leaves are crisp and the centre is tender.

Meanwhile, make the sauce. Scoop the avocado flesh into a food processor, add the fresh coriander, lemon zest and juice and tahini, and blend until smooth. Add the measured water and blend again to make a pourable sauce, then season to taste.

Serve 2 cabbage wedges per person on a bed of brown rice, drizzled with the sauce and with lemon wedges on the side for squeezing.

SERVES 4
Preparation time 15 minutes
Cooking time 30 minutes

SPICY BEAN BURGERS

450 g (14½ oz) sweet potatoes,
  peeled and cut into cubes
1 teaspoon olive oil, plus extra
  for brushing
400 g (13 oz) can black beans,
  drained and rinsed
1 tablespoon chipotle paste
finely grated zest and juice of
  ½ lime
2 tablespoons chopped fresh
  coriander
salt and pepper

To serve
4 vegan burger buns, halved
  and toasted
handful of mixed salad leaves
4 large slices of tomato
4 slices of red onion
4 tablespoons vegan
  mayonnaise
1 avocado, stoned, peeled and
  sliced

Toss the sweet potatoes in the oil. Cook in a preheated air fryer
at 180°C (350°F) for 20 minutes, until tender. Cool slightly.

Place the black beans, sweet potatoes, chipotle paste, lime zest and
juice, fresh coriander and a good sprinkling of salt and pepper in a food
processor and pulse until the mixture is roughly combined. Shape the
mixture into 4 burgers, then brush each with a little oil.

Cook the burgers in a preheated air fryer at 180°C (350°F) for
10 minutes, turning halfway through.

Top each bun base with some salad leaves and a slice of tomato
and onion. Add the burgers and serve topped with the mayonnaise,
avocado slices and bun tops.

LIGHT BITES & SIDES

MAKES 8
Preparation time 10 minutes
Cooking time 10 minutes

COURGETTE, SWEETCORN & CHILLI FRITTERS

1 large courgette, coarsely grated

75 g (3 oz) drained canned sweetcorn

1 red chilli, deseeded and finely chopped

2 tablespoons chopped mint

50 g (2 oz) self-raising flour

1 egg, lightly beaten

50 g (2 oz) ricotta cheese

olive oil, for spritzing

salt and pepper

To serve

sweet chilli sauce

crisp green salad

Squeeze the grated courgette in a clean tea towel to remove excess water, then place in a large bowl. Add the sweetcorn, chilli, mint and flour, then stir in the egg. Mix well and season with salt and pepper. Gently fold in the ricotta.

Place heaped tablespoons of the batter on a piece of pierced nonstick baking paper in a preheated air fryer, flatten slightly with the back of a spoon and spritz with oil. Cook at 190°C (375°F) for 6 minutes. Flip over and cook for a further 3—4 minutes, until golden. You may need to do this in 2 batches to make 8 in total.

Serve 2 fritters per person, drizzled with a little sweet chilli sauce, with a crisp green salad on the side.

SERVES 4–6
Preparation time 10 minutes
Cooking time 12 minutes

HALLOUMI STICKS WITH SPICY DIPPING SAUCE

2 x 225 g (7½ oz) packs vegetarian halloumi cheese
4 tablespoons plain flour
½ teaspoon dried oregano
½ teaspoon smoked paprika
½ teaspoon garlic powder
sunflower oil, for spritzing
pepper

Spicy dipping sauce
150 ml (5 fl oz) Greek yogurt
finely grated zest of ½ lemon
1 tablespoon harissa paste

Cut the halloumi into sticks about 1.5 cm (¾ inch) thick. On a plate, mix together the flour, oregano, paprika and garlic powder and season with pepper. Add the halloumi sticks and turn to coat in the flour.

Place half the halloumi sticks in a single layer in a preheated air fryer, spritz with a little oil and cook at 180°C (350°F) for 6 minutes, turning halfway through, until golden and crispy. Repeat with the remaining halloumi sticks.

Meanwhile, mix the yogurt for the dipping sauce with the lemon zest and swirl through the harissa paste. Serve the halloumi sticks immediately with the dip.

KALE CRISPS

200 g (7 oz) kale
2 teaspoons olive oil
25 g (1 oz) vegetarian Italian-
  style hard cheese, grated
½ teaspoon salt

Cut the kale leaves away from the spines, then cut into 3.5 cm (1½ inch) pieces. Place in a large bowl and drizzle over the oil. Use your hands to make sure the leaves are coated, then sprinkle over the cheese and salt and toss to coat.

Cook in batches in a single layer in a preheated air fryer at 190°C (375°F) for 3–5 minutes, checking them after 3 minutes and transferring any that are crisp to a wire rack. These are best eaten the day they are made.

SERVES 4
Preparation time 2 minutes
Cooking time 5 minutes

GOATS' CHEESE TOASTS WITH WALNUTS, THYME & HONEY

4 small slices of walnut bread
1 garlic clove, peeled
400 g (13 oz) piece of soft vegetarian goats' cheese with rind
2 teaspoons chopped thyme leaves
4 walnut halves, roughly chopped
4 teaspoons honey
pepper

To serve
watercress
cherry tomatoes

Cook the walnut bread in a preheated air fryer at 180°C (350°F) for 2 minutes, turning halfway through, until lightly toasted. You may need to do this in 2 batches. Rub the toast all over with the garlic clove.

Cut the round of goats' cheese into 4 slices, each about 1.5 cm (¾ inch) thick. Place each slice in the centre of a piece of toast and sprinkle with the thyme leaves, walnuts and pepper. Return to the air fryer and cook for 2–3 minutes, until the cheese starts to melt.

Drizzle with the honey and serve immediately with watercress and halved cherry tomatoes.

SERVES 4
Preparation time 8 minutes
Cooking time 30 minutes

SWEET POTATO & BEAN NACHOS

2 sweet potatoes, peeled and
    cut into 2.5 mm (⅛ inch) thick
    slices
2 teaspoons sunflower oil
2 teaspoons Mexican spice mix
200 g (7 oz) canned refried
    beans
4 tablespoons ready-made
    tomato salsa
8–12 jalapeño slices from a jar
50 g (2 oz) vegetarian
    mozzarella, grated
salt and pepper

To serve
soured cream
chopped chives
ready-made guacamole

Place the sweet potato slices in a bowl, drizzle over the oil, add the spice mix and salt and pepper and toss to coat. Cook half the slices in a single layer in a preheated air fryer at 180°C (350°F) for 10–12 minutes, turning once, until starting to crisp, removing any that are cooked. Repeat with the remaining sweet potato slices.

Arrange the sweet potato nachos in the base of an ovenproof dish, spoon over the beans, then add the salsa and jalapeños and sprinkle with the cheese.

Place the dish in the air fryer and cook for 4–5 minutes, until the cheese is melted and golden. Serve immediately with soured cream sprinkled with chopped chives and guacamole.

MAKES 14
Preparation time 20 minutes, plus chilling and freezing
Cooking time 30 minutes

MACARONI CHEESE BITES

125 g (4 oz) dried macaroni
25 g (1 oz) butter
25 g (1 oz) plain flour
300 ml (½ pint) milk
75 g (3 oz) mature vegetarian
    Cheddar cheese, grated
¼ teaspoon English mustard
    powder
sunflower oil, for spritzing
salt and pepper
ready-made pizza sauce,
    to serve

To coat
2 eggs
2 tablespoons milk
75 g (3 oz) panko breadcrumbs
2 teaspoons smoked paprika
1 teaspoon onion powder

Cook the macaroni in a saucepan of lightly salted boiling water according to the packet instructions, until just tender. Drain well.

Meanwhile, place the butter, flour and milk in a saucepan over a medium heat and cook, whisking continuously, for 3–5 minutes, until you have a thick sauce. Stir in the cheese and mustard powder, season to taste and simmer gently until the cheese has melted. Stir in the macaroni, cover and leave to cool, then chill in the refrigerator until ready to prepare.

Line a baking tray with nonstick baking paper, then use your hands or an ice cream scoop to roll the macaroni mixture into about 14 balls.

Place the eggs and milk for coating in a shallow bowl and whisk together. In another bowl, place the breadcrumbs, paprika and onion powder, season with a little salt and pepper and stir well.

Dip the balls in the egg mixture to fully coat, then roll in the breadcrumbs and arrange on the baking tray. Place in the freezer for 30 minutes.

Place half the balls in a single layer in a preheated air fryer, spritz with oil and cook at 180°C (350°F) for 5 minutes. Turn the balls over, spritz with a little more oil and cook for a further 4–5 minutes, until golden. Repeat with the remaining macaroni cheese bites, then serve with pizza sauce, for dipping.

MAKES 4
Preparation time 5 minutes
Cooking time 25 minutes

YORKSHIRE PUDDINGS

50 g (2 oz) plain flour
pinch of salt
4 tablespoons milk
4 tablespoons water
1 large egg
2 teaspoons sunflower oil

Place the flour and salt in a bowl and mix together the milk and measured water in a jug. Using a whisk, gradually add the egg and a little of the milk mixture to the flour, whisking to incorporate, then add the remaining liquid, until you have a smooth batter. Transfer the mixture to a jug.

Divide the oil between 4 metal pudding tins or ramekins, about 150 ml (¼ pint) capacity each, then brush it up the sides. Place the tins in a preheated air fryer at 200°C (400°F) for 5 minutes to heat.

Pour the mixture into the tins and cook for 20 minutes, without opening the drawer. The Yorkshires will be risen and golden brown. Serve immediately.

SERVES 3–4
Preparation time 5 minutes
Cooking time 18 minutes

HONEY & THYME ROASTED ROOTS

325 g (11 oz) parsnips, peeled
　and cut into 3.5 cm (1½ inch)
　pieces
325 g (11 oz) Chantenay carrots,
　halved if large
1 tablespoon olive oil
2 tablespoons honey
2 thyme sprigs
salt and pepper

Place the parsnips and carrots in a bowl, add the oil, honey and thyme, season to taste and stir well to coat.

Cook in a preheated air fryer at 180°C (350°F) for 15–18 minutes, turning halfway through and brushing with any remaining mixture in the bowl, until caramelized and tender.

SERVES 2–3
Preparation time 2 minutes
Cooking time 16 minutes

CRISPY SESAME NOODLES

125 g (4 oz) dried medium egg
noodles
2 teaspoons sesame oil
2 teaspoons grated fresh root
ginger
½ teaspoon salt
150 g (5 oz) bean sprouts

To serve
4 spring onions, thinly sliced
2 teaspoons sesame seeds

Cook the noodles in a saucepan of boiling water according to the packet instructions, until just tender, then drain well.

Place in a bowl, add the oil, ginger and salt and toss well. Cook on a piece of pierced nonstick baking paper in a preheated air fryer at 190°C (375°F) for 7 minutes, until starting to crisp. Add the bean sprouts, stir well and cook for a further 5 minutes, until all the noodles are crispy.

Meanwhile, place the sesame seeds in a dry frying pan over a medium heat, stirring occasionally, until lightly toasted.

Serve immediately, sprinkled with the spring onions and toasted sesame seeds.

SERVES 2–3
Preparation time 5 minutes
Cooking time 21 minutes

VEGETABLE EGG 'FRIED' RICE

1 teaspoon sunflower oil

1 carrot, finely diced

½ small red pepper, cored, deseeded and chopped

1 head of pak choi, white stalks sliced and leaves halved if large

250 g (8 oz) cooked long-grain rice

2 spring onions, chopped

1 teaspoon toasted sesame oil

1 large egg, beaten

75 g (3 oz) frozen peas, defrosted

1 tablespoon light soy sauce

Place the sunflower oil in a 20 cm (8 inch) round cake tin or ovenproof dish. Place in a preheated air fryer at 180°C (350°F) for 2 minutes to heat up. Add the carrot, red pepper and pak choi stalks, stir to coat in the oil, then cook for 4 minutes, stirring halfway through.

Meanwhile, place the rice and spring onions in a bowl, add the sesame oil and stir to coat. Add the rice to the vegetables and stir well, then cook for a further 10 minutes, stirring halfway through.

Add the egg to the top of the rice and cook for 3 minutes until just set. Break up the egg with a fork, stir in the peas, pak choi leaves and soy sauce, then cook for a further 2 minutes. Serve immediately.

SERVES 4
Preparation time 15 minutes
Cooking time 38 minutes

CHEESY GRATIN POTATOES

butter, for greasing
450 g (14½ oz) potatoes, peeled
150 ml (¼ pint) double cream
150 ml (¼ pint) milk
2 garlic cloves, crushed
pinch of grated nutmeg
25 g (1 oz) mature vegetarian
   Cheddar cheese, grated
salt and pepper

Grease a 17 cm (6½ inch) square ovenproof dish. Slice the potatoes to about 2.5 mm (⅛ inch) thick and layer them in the dish.

Place the cream, milk, garlic, nutmeg and salt and pepper in a saucepan over a medium heat and bring to the boil. Pour over the potatoes in the dish. Place the dish in a preheated air fryer and cook at 150°C (300°F) for 30 minutes, stirring gently every 10 minutes, until tender.

Sprinkle over the cheese, increase the temperature to 180°C (350°F) and cook for a further 4–5 minutes, until the topping is golden. Allow to stand for a few minutes for the cream to thicken before serving.

SERVES 2–3
Preparation time 4 minutes
Cooking time 9 minutes

BALSAMIC ASPARAGUS & TENDERSTEM BROCCOLI

200 g (7 oz) asparagus spears, woody stems removed
150 g (5 oz) Tenderstem broccoli, stalks trimmed
1 teaspoon olive oil
1 teaspoon balsamic vinegar
15 g (½ oz) vegetarian Italian-style hard cheese, to serve
salt and pepper

Place the asparagus spears and broccoli in a bowl, add the oil, vinegar and salt and pepper and toss well.

Cook the asparagus in a single layer in a preheated air fryer at 190°C (375°F) for 4 minutes, then turn the asparagus and add the broccoli. Cook for a further 4–5 minutes, until tender and starting to crisp.

Place in a serving dish and use a vegetable peeler to shave the Italian-style hard cheese over the top. Serve immediately.

SERVES 4
Preparation time 5 minutes, plus cooling
Cooking time 20 minutes

CRISPY SALT & PEPPER CHICKPEAS

400 g (13 oz) can chickpeas, drained and rinsed
2 teaspoons olive oil
1 teaspoon sea salt
1 teaspoon freshly ground black pepper

Dry the chickpeas on kitchen paper to remove any excess water, then remove any loose skins.

Mix together the oil, salt and pepper in a bowl, add the chickpeas and toss in the mixture to ensure they are evenly coated.

Cook in a preheated air fryer at 200°C (400°F) for 15–20 minutes, shaking the basket occasionally, until crispy. Allow to cool as they will continue to crisp. Serve as a snack or as a salad topper.

SERVES 4
Preparation time 15 minutes
Cooking time 16 minutes

SPICED TORTILLA CHIPS WITH MANGO & LIME DIPPING SAUCE

6 mini corn or flour tortillas
2 teaspoons sunflower oil
1 tablespoon Mexican spice mix
salt and pepper

Dipping sauce
1 large mango, peeled and
   pitted
1 tablespoon olive oil
finely grated zest and juice of
   ½ lime
1 red jalapeño chilli, deseeded
   and finely chopped
2 tablespoons finely chopped
   fresh coriander

To serve
ready-made guacamole
ready-made salsa

Brush both sides of the tortillas with a little oil, then sprinkle over some spice mix and season with a little salt and pepper.

Stack the tortillas on top of each other and cut into 6, so you have 36 tortilla chips.

Separate out the tortillas and cook half in a preheated air fryer at 160°C (325°F) for 6 minutes, shaking halfway through. Remove any chips that are golden, then cook the remainder for a further 1–2 minutes until golden. Transfer to a wire rack – they will continue to crisp as they cool. Cook the remaining tortillas in the same way.

Meanwhile, finely chop one-third of the mango and set aside. Roughly chop the rest and place in a small food processor with the oil, lime zest and juice and chilli and blitz until smooth, or use a stick blender. Transfer to a bowl and stir in the reserved mango and fresh coriander. Season to taste and serve the tortillas with the dipping sauce and some ready-made guacamole and salsa.

SERVES 4
Preparation time 15 minutes, plus cooling
Cooking time 12 minutes

ROASTED CAULIFLOWER TABBOULEH

½ cauliflower, cut into 2.5 cm (1 inch) florets
2 teaspoons olive oil
1 teaspoon Baharat or Middle Eastern spice mix
100 g (3½ oz) bulgur wheat
300 g (10 oz) tomatoes, finely chopped
¼ cucumber, deseeded and diced
5 spring onions, thinly sliced
150 g (5 oz) pomegranate seeds
6 tablespoons chopped flat leaf parsley
4 tablespoons chopped mint

Dressing
2 tablespoons olive oil
juice of 1 lemon
salt and pepper

Place the cauliflower florets in a bowl, drizzle over the oil, sprinkle over the spice mix and toss well to coat. Cook in a preheated air fryer at 180°C (350°F) for 12 minutes, shaking the basket a couple of times, until crisp.

Meanwhile, place the bulgur wheat in a saucepan of lightly salted cold water, bring to the boil and simmer for 8–10 minutes, until tender. Drain well, then spread out on a baking sheet to cool.

Place the cooled bulgur wheat and cauliflower in a bowl, then gently stir in the tomatoes, cucumber, spring onions, pomegranate seeds and herbs.

Whisk together the dressing ingredients, pour over the tabbouleh, mix well and serve immediately.

SERVES 4
Preparation time 20 minutes, plus chilling
Cooking time 10 minutes

FALAFEL BOWLS

400 g (13 oz) can chickpeas,
   drained and rinsed
1 garlic clove, crushed
1 teaspoon ground cumin
½ teaspoon ground coriander
2 tablespoons chopped flat leaf
   parsley
½ teaspoon salt
1 teaspoon baking powder
1 tablespoon plain flour
1 tablespoon lemon juice
2 teaspoons olive oil, plus extra
   for spritzing
pepper

Tahini dressing
4 tablespoons tahini
juice of ½ lemon
4 tablespoons cold water

To serve
250 g (8 oz) cooked quinoa
2 carrots, grated
4 tomatoes, quartered
½ cucumber, deseeded and
   chopped

Place the chickpeas, garlic, spices, parsley and salt in a food processor, season with pepper and pulse until coarsely chopped. Add the baking powder, flour, lemon juice and oil and pulse until well combined.

Divide the mixture into 12 and roll into balls, then flatten slightly. Cover and chill in the refrigerator for 30 minutes.

Place in a preheated air fryer, spritz with a little oil and cook at 180°C (350°F) for 10 minutes, turning halfway through.

Meanwhile, mix together the dressing ingredients and season to taste. Divide the quinoa, carrots, tomatoes and cucumber between 4 bowls. Top each bowl with 3 falafel and drizzle over the tahini dressing.

MAKES 16
Preparation time 20 minutes, plus resting
Cooking time 24 minutes

VEGETABLE SAMOSAS

75 g (3 oz) potato, peeled and
   cut into 1 cm (½ inch) dice
1 onion, cut into 1 cm (½ inch)
   dice
1 small carrot, cut into 1 cm
   (½ inch) dice
2 teaspoons sunflower oil
1 teaspoon cumin seeds
50 g (2 oz) frozen peas,
   defrosted
1 tablespoon medium curry
   paste
2 tablespoons chopped fresh
   coriander, plus extra leaves
   to garnish
salt and pepper
mango chutney, to serve

Pastry
225 g (7½ oz) plain flour, plus
   extra for dusting
1 teaspoon salt
2 tablespoons sunflower oil, plus
   extra for spritzing
100 ml (3½ fl oz) cold water

Mix the flour and salt for the pastry in a bowl. Make a well in the centre and add the oil. Using your hands, mix the ingredients to form crumbs. Gradually add the measured water to make a firm dough. Transfer to a lightly floured surface and knead the dough for 5–10 minutes, until smooth. Roll into a ball, place in a plastic food bag and set aside at room temperature for 30 minutes.

Place the potato, onion, carrot, oil and cumin seeds in an ovenproof dish, season with salt and pepper and mix well. Place the dish in a preheated air fryer and cook at 180°C (350°F) for 10 minutes, until just tender. Transfer to a bowl, stir in the peas, curry paste and coriander and gently mix. Leave to cool.

Divide the dough into 8 equal pieces, then roll one out to a 15 cm (6 inch) disc. Cut in half to make 2 semi-circles. Brush the straight edge of one with a little water, then fold one corner to the centre of the curved edge and bring the other corner up over the top to make a cone. Fill the cone with a tablespoon of the filling and seal the open edges together with a little water. Repeat with the remaining filling and dough.

Place half the samosas in a single layer in a preheated air fryer, spritz with oil and cook at 180°C (350°F) for 10–12 minutes, turning halfway through, until golden. Repeat with the remaining samosas. Garnish with coriander leaves and serve with mango chutney.

SERVES 4–6
Preparation time 10 minutes
Cooking time 15 minutes

ROASTED RED PEPPER & WALNUT DIP WITH PITTA CHIPS

2 large red peppers, cored, deseeded and quartered
75 g (3 oz) walnuts
juice of ½ lemon
1 tablespoon pomegranate molasses
½ teaspoon chilli paste
1 teaspoon olive oil
salt and pepper

Pitta chips
4 mini vegan pitta breads
2 teaspoons olive oil
1 teaspoon salt
1 teaspoon freshly ground black pepper

To garnish
pomegranate seeds
mint leaves

Cook the red pepper pieces, skin side up, in a preheated air fryer at 200°C (400°F) for 8–10 minutes, until the skin is blackened. Place in a plastic food bag and allow to cool slightly. When the peppers are cool enough to handle, remove and discard the blackened skins, then place the pieces on kitchen paper to remove excess moisture.

Meanwhile, place the walnuts in a dry frying pan over a medium heat, stirring occasionally, until lightly toasted. Transfer to a food processor and blend until finely ground, then add the peppers, lemon juice, pomegranate molasses, chilli paste and oil. Blend until smooth, then season to taste.

For the pitta chips, cut each pitta into 6 triangles, then place in a bowl and drizzle over the oil. Sprinkle with the salt and pepper and toss until evenly coated. Cook in a single layer in a preheated air fryer at 180°C (350°F) for 4 minutes, turning once, until crisp. You may need to do this in 2 batches.

Place the dip in a bowl and garnish with pomegranate seeds and mint leaves. Serve with the pitta chips for dipping.

SERVES 2
Preparation time 10–12 minutes
Cooking time 8 minutes

CREAMY MISO MUSHROOMS ON SOURDOUGH

2 teaspoons white or brown
  miso paste
1 teaspoon dark soy sauce
1 garlic clove, crushed
2 teaspoons olive oil
200 g (7 oz) mushrooms, such
  as chestnut or Portobello,
  roughly chopped
4 tablespoons vegan cream
2 slices of sourdough bread
pepper
2 tablespoons chopped flat leaf
  parsley, to garnish

Mix the miso paste, soy sauce, garlic and oil in a large bowl and season well with pepper. Add the mushrooms and turn to coat, then transfer to an ovenproof dish.

Place the dish in a preheated air fryer and cook at 180°C (350°F) for 7 minutes, stirring once. Stir in the cream, then return to the air fryer and cook for 1 minute to heat through.

Cook the bread in a preheated air fryer at 180°C (350°F) for 2 minutes, turning halfway through, until lightly toasted. You may need to do this in 2 batches.

Spoon the mushrooms over the toast and sprinkle over the parsley. Serve immediately.

SERVES 4
Preparation time 10 minutes
Cooking time 28 minutes

CHILLI & PAPRIKA VEGETABLE CRISPS

1 small sweet potato, scrubbed
1 beetroot, scrubbed
1 parsnip, scrubbed
2 teaspoons chilli-flavoured oil
2 teaspoons smoked paprika,
   plus extra for sprinkling
1 teaspoon sea salt

Slice the vegetables thinly, using a mandolin or a sharp knife, to about 2.5 mm (⅛ inch) thick. Place in a large bowl, add the oil and turn to coat the vegetables, then add the paprika and salt and toss to coat.

Cook half the vegetable slices in a single layer in a preheated air fryer at 150°C (300°F) for 12 minutes, turning halfway through. Remove any crisps that are golden, then cook the remainder for a further 1–2 minutes, until golden. Transfer to a wire rack – they will continue to crisp as they cool. Repeat with the remaining vegetable slices in the same way.

Sprinkle the crisps with a little extra paprika before serving.

SERVES 4
Preparation time 10 minutes
Cooking time 20 minutes

FLAVOUR-BOMB POTATOES

550 g (1 lb 2 oz) potatoes,
   peeled and cut into 2 cm
   (¾ inch) pieces
1 tablespoon sunflower oil
1 tablespoon grated fresh root
   ginger
1 teaspoon cumin seeds
1 teaspoon garlic powder
1 teaspoon onion powder
1 teaspoon black mustard seeds
½ teaspoon ground turmeric
2 teaspoons ground coriander
1 teaspoon garam masala
1 teaspoon hot chilli powder
2 tomatoes, roughly chopped
½ teaspoon salt
pepper
large handful of chopped fresh
   coriander, to garnish

Place the potatoes in a large bowl, add all the remaining ingredients and stir well to coat.

Cook in a preheated air fryer at 190°C (375°F) for 20 minutes, shaking halfway through, until the potatoes are tender. Sprinkle with the fresh coriander and serve immediately.

SERVES 2–3
Preparation time 5 minutes
Cooking time 26 minutes

SWEET POTATO FRIES

2 sweet potatoes, scrubbed

2 teaspoons olive oil

½ teaspoon sea salt

4 teaspoons cornmeal or
    polenta

ketchup, to serve

Cut the sweet potatoes into 1 cm (½ inch) thick fries. Rinse in cold water, then pat dry on kitchen paper or in a clean tea towel.

Place in a bowl, drizzle over the oil and sprinkle with the salt and cornmeal or polenta. Toss the fries until evenly coated.

Cook half the fries in a single layer in a preheated air fryer at 190°C (375°F) for 10–12 minutes, shaking once. Repeat with the remaining fries, then return them all to the basket and cook for 2 minutes, until hot and crispy. Serve immediately with ketchup.

SERVES 4
Preparation time 5 minutes, plus chilling
Cooking time 20 minutes

PERFECT CHIPS

4 large floury potatoes, such as Maris Piper or King Edward, peeled
2 teaspoons olive oil
½ teaspoon salt

Cut the potatoes into 1.5 cm (¾ inch) thick chips. Place in a bowl and cover with cold water, then chill in the refrigerator for 30 minutes.

Drain the chips and pat dry, then place in a bowl and toss with the oil and salt.

Cook in a preheated air fryer at 160°C (325°F) for 12 minutes, shaking halfway through. Increase the temperature to 200°C (400°F) and cook for a further 8 minutes, shaking occasionally, until golden and crisp. Do not overfill the air fryer or the chips won't cook evenly – you may need to do this in 2 batches. If so, return all the chips to the air fryer at the end and cook for a further 2 minutes. Serve immediately.

SERVES 4
Preparation time 10 minutes
Cooking time 27 minutes

PERFECT ROAST POTATOES

1 kg (2 lb) floury potatoes, such as Maris Piper or King Edward, peeled
2 tablespoons olive oil
1 teaspoon sea salt
2 rosemary sprigs (optional)

Cut the potatoes into even-sized pieces, about 3.5 cm (1½ inches) across. Cook in a saucepan of lightly salted boiling water for 7 minutes, then drain in a colander and leave to steam dry for 3 minutes.

Shake the colander to rough up the edges of the potatoes – this helps make them extra crispy. Place the potatoes in a bowl, add the olive oil, salt and rosemary, if using, and turn to coat in the oil.

Cook in a preheated air fryer at 200°C (400°F) for 20 minutes, turning halfway through, then shaking the basket once more, until golden and crispy. Serve immediately.

SWEET
TREATS

SERVES 8
Preparation time 15 minutes, plus chilling
Cooking time 40 minutes

BAKED LEMON CURD CHEESECAKE

50 g (2 oz) butter, plus extra for
    greasing
200 g (7 oz) ginger biscuits,
    crushed
400 g (13 oz) cream cheese
75 g (3 oz) caster sugar
250 g (8 oz) lemon curd
100 ml (3½ fl oz) soured cream
3 eggs
50 g (2 oz) plain flour
lemon zest, to decorate

Grease and line the base of an 18 cm (7 inch) springform cake tin with
nonstick baking paper. Melt the butter in a saucepan, then stir in the
crushed biscuits and press into the base of the tin in an even layer.
Chill in the refrigerator while you make the filling.

Place the cream cheese, sugar and 200 g (7 oz) of the lemon curd in
a bowl and whisk until smooth. Whisk in the soured cream and eggs,
then fold in the flour and pour the mixture over the biscuit base.

Cook in a preheated air fryer at 150°C (300°F) for 35–40 minutes, until
the sides are set but the middle is still slightly wobbly. Cover the top
with foil if it becomes too brown. Allow to cool at room temperature,
then chill in the refrigerator for at least 4 hours or overnight.

Spread the top with the reserved lemon curd and decorate with lemon
zest just before serving.

SERVES 2
Preparation time 10 minutes
Cooking time 14 minutes

BANANAS WITH MISO CARAMEL SAUCE

25 g (1 oz) unsalted butter
25 g (1 oz) light soft brown sugar
1 tablespoon golden syrup
3 tablespoons double cream
1–2 teaspoons white miso paste
50 g (2 oz) plain flour
125 ml (4 fl oz) cold water
25 g (1 oz) panko breadcrumbs
2 bananas, cut in half
sunflower oil, for spritzing
ice cream, to serve

Place the butter, sugar and syrup in a small saucepan. Melt over a gentle heat, stirring until the sugar has dissolved. Add the cream and miso paste and boil for 3–4 minutes, until thickened. Allow to cool slightly.

Meanwhile, place the flour in a bowl and gradually add the measured water, whisking so there are no lumps, until you have a thick batter the consistency of double cream.

Place the breadcrumbs in a shallow bowl, dunk each banana half in the batter to fully coat, then roll in the breadcrumbs.

Spritz generously with oil, then cook in a preheated air fryer at 200°C (400°F) for 6–8 minutes, turning once, until golden and crispy. Serve immediately with a scoop of ice cream topped with the warm miso caramel sauce.

MAKES 4
Preparation time 10 minutes, plus cooling
Cooking time 15 minutes

CAPPUCCINO CUPCAKES

50 g (2 oz) self-raising flour
1 tablespoon cocoa powder,
    sifted, plus extra for dusting
50 g (2 oz) unsalted butter,
    softened
50 g (2 oz) caster sugar
1 egg, beaten
2 teaspoons instant coffee,
    dissolved in 1 tablespoon
    boiling water

Vanilla buttercream
50 g (2 oz) unsalted butter,
    softened
150 g (5 oz) icing sugar, sifted
½ teaspoon vanilla extract

Line 4 small cake tins or ramekins with paper muffin cases. Place all the cake ingredients in a bowl and beat with an electric whisk until combined.

Divide the mixture between the paper cases and level the tops. Place the tins in a preheated air fryer and cook at 160°C (325°F) for 13–15 minutes, until springy to the touch. Allow to cool for a few minutes, then transfer to a wire rack to cool completely.

Place the butter for the icing in a bowl and gradually beat in the icing sugar a little at a time. Once all the sugar has been added, add the vanilla and beat together. Pipe or spoon the buttercream on the cakes and decorate with a dusting of cocoa powder.

MAKES 16
Preparation time 10 minutes
Cooking time 28 minutes

CHOCOLATE BROWNIES

125 g (4 oz) unsalted butter,
  cut into cubes, plus extra for
  greasing
75 g (3 oz) cocoa powder
2 eggs
225 g (7½ oz) granulated sugar
1 teaspoon vanilla extract
pinch of salt
50 g (2 oz) plain flour

Grease and line the base and sides of a 15 cm (6 inch) square cake tin, about 5 cm (2 inches) deep, with nonstick baking paper.

Place the butter and cocoa powder in a small saucepan over a low heat, stirring frequently until the butter has melted. Remove from the heat and leave to cool for 3–4 minutes.

Meanwhile, in a large bowl, whisk together the eggs, sugar, vanilla and salt with an electric whisk for about 2 minutes, until pale and thick. Add the cocoa and butter mixture and whisk to combine.

Sift the flour over the mixture and mix thoroughly, then pour into the prepared tin and level the top. Place the tin in a preheated air fryer and cook at 160°C (325°F) for 23–25 minutes, until just firm to the touch and a wooden cocktail stick inserted in the middle comes out with moist crumbs. Leave to cool in the tin before cutting into squares.

MAKES 6
Preparation time 10 minutes
Cooking time 10 minutes

FRUITY OLIVE OIL SCONES

225 g (7½ oz) self-raising flour,
  plus extra for dusting
1 teaspoon baking powder
25 g (1 oz) caster sugar
50 g (2 oz) mixed dried fruit
1 egg
50 ml (2 fl oz) mild olive oil
5 tablespoons milk, plus extra
  for brushing

To serve
strawberry jam
clotted cream

Place the flour, baking powder, sugar and dried fruit in a large bowl. Stir well to combine.

Crack the egg into a measuring jug, then beat in the olive oil and milk. Stir the mixture into the flour and mix to a soft, sticky dough. Turn out on to a lightly floured surface, knead lightly and roll out to about 2.5 cm (1 inch) thick.

Cut into 6 rounds with a fluted 6 cm (2½ inch) cutter, using the trimmings as necessary to make more scones. Place on a piece of pierced nonstick baking paper in a preheated air fryer, brush the tops of the scones with a little extra milk and cook at 180°C (350°F) for 5 minutes.

Turn the scones over and cook for a further 5 minutes, or until well risen and golden brown. Transfer to a wire rack to cool.

To serve, split the scones and serve with strawberry jam and a good dollop of clotted cream.

SERVES 4
Preparation time 10 minutes, plus freezing
Cooking time 5 minutes

CRUNCHY ICE CREAM BALLS WITH CHOCOLATE FUDGE SAUCE

4 scoops of vanilla ice cream
75 g (3 oz) cinnamon crunch
   cereal or cornflakes
2 egg whites
sunflower oil, for spritzing

Chocolate fudge sauce
200 ml (7 fl oz) condensed milk
25 g (1 oz) unsalted butter
75 g (3 oz) dark chocolate
   chunks

Line a baking sheet with nonstick baking paper. Place the ice cream balls on the tray and freeze for 2 hours.

Meanwhile, place the cereal in a food processor and pulse to a crumb. Place in a shallow dish. Whisk the egg whites until frothy.

Remove the ice cream from the freezer and dip the balls into the egg whites, then roll in the crumb mixture, coating completely. Reserve the remaining egg whites and crumbs. Freeze the ice cream balls for another hour, then dip again in the egg whites and coat again in the crumbs. Return to the freezer for at least 1 hour.

Make the chocolate fudge sauce when ready to serve. Place all the ingredients in a small saucepan over a low heat and stir until the chocolate and butter have melted.

Meanwhile, place the balls on a piece of pierced nonstick baking paper in a preheated air fryer, spritz with a little oil and cook at 200°C (400°F) for 2 minutes. Serve immediately with the warm fudge sauce.

SERVES 4–6
Preparation time 10 minutes
Cooking time 30 minutes

PEAR & SALTED CARAMEL TARTE TATIN

4 pears, peeled, cored and
  halved
4 tablespoons salted caramel
  sauce from a jar
250 g (8 oz) ready-made puff
  pastry
plain flour, for dusting
vanilla ice cream, to serve
  (optional)

Spoon the caramel sauce into the base of an 18 cm (7 inch) round
ovenproof dish or cake tin and spread evenly. Arrange the pears
snugly in the dish, cut sides up.

Roll out the pastry on a lightly floured surface to 3 mm (⅛ inch) thick.
Cut out a disc 1 cm (½ inch) wider than your dish, place on top of the
pears and tuck in around the edges. Prick the pastry all over with
a fork and pierce a hole in the centre to help the steam escape.

Place the dish in a preheated air fryer at 180°C (350°F) and cook for
25–30 minutes, until well risen and golden. Cool for 10 minutes, then
carefully invert on to a large plate and serve warm, in slices, with vanilla
ice cream, if you like.

MAKES 4
Preparation time 10 minutes, plus cooling
Cooking time 15 minutes

BLUEBERRY & LEMON MUFFINS

3 tablespoons sunflower or light
   olive oil

1 egg

3 tablespoons milk

finely grated zest of 1 lemon

1 tablespoon lemon juice

125 g (4 oz) plain flour

1 teaspoon baking powder

½ teaspoon salt

3 tablespoons caster sugar

75 g (3 oz) blueberries, plus
   extra to decorate

Lemon icing

4 tablespoons icing sugar

1 teaspoon finely grated lemon
   zest, plus extra to decorate

1 teaspoon lemon juice

Line 4 small cake tins or ramekins with paper muffin cases. In a jug, whisk together the oil, egg, milk, lemon zest and juice.

Stir the flour, baking powder, salt and sugar together in a bowl, then stir the wet ingredients into the dry ingredients until just combined. Stir in the blueberries.

Divide the mixture between the cases and place the tins in a preheated air fryer. Cook at 160°C (325°F) for 14–15 minutes, until springy to the touch. Allow to cool on a wire rack.

Make the icing by mixing all the ingredients together, then spoon over the cooled muffins and top with some extra blueberries and lemon zest.

SERVES 2
Preparation time 5 minutes
Cooking time 24 minutes

APPLE & CINNAMON CRISPS

2 dessert apples
1 teaspoon ground cinnamon

Cut the apples into 2.5 mm (⅛ inch) thick slices using a mandolin or sharp knife and remove any seeds.

Place In a bowl, sprinkle over the cinnamon and toss well to coat evenly. Cook half the slices in a single layer in a preheated air fryer at 150°C (300°F) for 10–12 minutes, turning halfway through, until crisp.

Transfer to a wire rack to cool and continue crisping, then repeat with the remaining apple slices. Store any leftover crisps in an airtight container for 1–2 days.

SERVES 2–4
Preparation time 5 minutes, plus marinating
Cooking time 10 minutes

MOJITO MANGO CHEEKS

2 tablespoons golden caster
   sugar
2 heaped tablespoons mint
   leaves, plus extra to decorate
finely grated zest and juice of
   1 lime
2 ripe mangoes
50 ml (2 fl oz) white rum

Place the sugar, mint leaves and lime zest in a small food processor and blend until you have bright green sugar. Set aside.

Slice the flesh off the mangoes either side of the stone, giving you 2 cheeks from each mango. Score a diamond pattern into the flesh on the cut side of each cheek, taking care not to cut through the skin. Place, cut sides up, in a shallow dish.

Combine the rum and lime juice in a small bowl and spoon 1 tablespoon of the liquid over each scored mango cheek, allowing it to drizzle into the cuts. Leave to marinate for 5–10 minutes, or until you are ready to serve.

Sprinkle 2 teaspoons of the mint sugar over each mango cheek, then cook on a piece of pierced nonstick baking paper in a preheated air fryer at 180°C (350°F) for 8–10 minutes, until starting to caramelize. Sprinkle with the remaining mint sugar and extra mint leaves and serve immediately.

MAKES 8
Preparation time 10 minutes, plus cooling
Cooking time 28 minutes

OAT COOKIES

75 g (3 oz) porridge oats
75 g (3 oz) desiccated coconut
75 g (3 oz) plain flour
pinch of salt
½ teaspoon bicarbonate of soda
½ teaspoon ground cinnamon
50 g (2 oz) vegan butter
100 g (3½ oz) light soft brown
   sugar
1 teaspoon vanilla extract
4 tablespoons golden syrup

Mix together the oats, coconut, flour, salt, bicarbonate of soda and cinnamon in a large bowl.

Place the butter, sugar and vanilla extract in a bowl and use an electric whisk to beat together until creamy. Beat in the golden syrup.

Stir in the dry ingredients to make a crumbly mixture. Use slightly damp hands to press and roll the mixture into 8 balls and flatten slightly.

Cook half the cookies spaced apart on a piece of pierced nonstick baking paper in a preheated air fryer at 150°C (300°F) for 12–14 minutes, until golden brown. They will still be soft in the middle but will firm up on cooling.

Allow to cool in the air fryer for 5 minutes, then transfer to a wire rack to cool completely. Repeat with the remaining cookies.

MAKES 8 SQUARES
Preparation time 8 minutes
Cooking time 20 minutes

STICKY GINGER CAKE

50 g (2 oz) vegan butter, melted,
    plus extra for greasing
75 g (3 oz) self-raising flour
1 tablespoon ground ginger
2 pieces of stem ginger from
    a jar, chopped, plus
    2 tablespoons of the syrup
1 teaspoon ground mixed spice
50 g (2 oz) light soft brown
    sugar
75 g (3 oz) golden syrup
50 ml (2 fl oz) plant-based milk

Grease and line the base of a 500 g (1 lb) loaf tin with nonstick baking paper.

Mix together the flour, ground ginger, chopped ginger pieces, mixed spice and sugar in a large bowl.

Whisk together the golden syrup, melted butter and milk in a jug, then pour over the dry ingredients and stir well. Pour into the prepared tin, place the tin in a preheated air fryer at 160°C (325°F) and cook for 20 minutes, until golden brown and risen and a skewer inserted into the middle comes out clean.

Prick the surface of the cake all over with a cocktail stick, then drizzle over the ginger syrup. Leave in the tin to cool, then remove and cut into 8 squares.

MAKES 14
Preparation time 10 minutes
Cooking time 28 minutes

AMARETTI BISCUITS

150 g (5 oz) ground almonds
125 g (4 oz) caster sugar
½ teaspoon baking powder
50 ml (2 fl oz) aquafaba (water
    from a can of chickpeas)
½ teaspoon lemon juice
1 teaspoon almond extract
2 tablespoons icing sugar

Mix together the ground almonds, caster sugar and baking powder in a bowl.

Place the aquafaba in a large clean bowl with the lemon juice and beat with an electric whisk for about 4–5 minutes, until the mixture forms stiff peaks.

Fold 2 tablespoons of the aquafaba into the ground almond mixture, then gently fold in the rest. Stir in the almond extract.

Roll the mixture into 14 balls, about 20 g (¾ oz) each. Place the icing sugar on a plate and roll the balls in the sugar to coat.

Cook half the amaretti spaced apart on a piece of pierced nonstick baking paper in a preheated air fryer at 160°C (325°F) for 14 minutes, until golden. Allow to cool in the air fryer for 2 minutes, then transfer to a wire rack to cool completely. Repeat with the remaining amaretti.

SERVES 4
Preparation time 10 minutes
Cooking time 18 minutes

MINI RHUBARB & ALMOND CRUMBLES

400 g (13 oz) rhubarb, cut into 2.5 cm (1 inch) lengths
75 g (3 oz) caster sugar
grated zest and juice of 1 small orange
100 g (3½ oz) plain flour
25 g (1 oz) jumbo oats
2 tablespoons flaked almonds, roughly chopped
4 tablespoons ground almonds
4 tablespoons light soft brown sugar
4 tablespoons melted coconut oil
plant-based custard, to serve

Place the rhubarb, caster sugar and orange juice in a large bowl and stir well. Set aside while you make the crumble.

Mix together the flour, oats, flaked and ground almonds, soft brown sugar and orange zest in a bowl. Stir in the coconut oil until the mixture comes together and resembles coarse crumbs.

Divide the rhubarb mixture with its juices between 4 ramekins, 150–200 ml (5–7 fl oz) capacity each. Sprinkle over the crumble topping, place the ramekins in a preheated air fryer at 180°C (350°F) and cook for 15–18 minutes, until golden and bubbling. Serve with plant-based custard.

SERVES 4
Preparation time 5 minutes
Cooking time 19 minutes

CHILLI CARAMEL POPCORN CLUSTERS

50 g (2 oz) sweet and salty
    popcorn
25 g (1 oz) pecans, chopped
25 g (1 oz) almonds, chopped
2 tablespoons mixed seeds,
    such as pumpkin, sunflower
    and linseed
2 tablespoons coconut oil
125 ml (4 fl oz) maple syrup
2 teaspoons dried chilli flakes

Mix together the popcorn, nuts and seeds in a large bowl.

Place the coconut oil, maple syrup and chilli flakes in a small saucepan over a low heat and stir for 2–3 minutes, until the coconut oil has melted. Bring to the boil and simmer for 4 minutes, until the liquid thickens slightly and darkens.

Pour over the popcorn mixture in the bowl and stir well so that everything is coated.

Place the mixture on a piece of pierced nonstick baking paper in a preheated air fryer, press together into clumps with the back of a spoon and cook at 120°C (250°F) for 12 minutes, stirring halfway through and pressing again with the back of a spoon, until golden. Allow to cool completely as the mixture will continue to harden.

Once cool, break any large pieces into clusters. Store in an airtight container for up to 1 week.

MAKES 6
Preparation time 15 minutes, plus cooling
Cooking time 20 minutes

JAM TURNOVERS WITH VANILLA CREAM

1 sheet of ready-rolled vegan
    puff pastry
plain flour, for dusting
6 tablespoons strawberry jam,
    or your favourite jam
plant-based milk, for brushing
caster sugar, for sprinkling
icing sugar, for dusting

Vanilla cream
250 ml (8 fl oz) whippable oat
    cream
1 teaspoon vanilla extract
1 tablespoon caster sugar

Unroll the puff pastry on a lightly floured surface. Cut it into 6 squares, about 10 cm (4 inches) across. Spoon 1 tablespoon of the jam into the centre of each pastry square.

Brush the edges of the squares with a little milk, fold over to make triangles, then seal the edges by pressing down with a fork. Brush the tops with milk and sprinkle with a little caster sugar.

Cook half the turnovers in a preheated air fryer at 190°C (375°F) for 8–10 minutes, until puffed and golden. Transfer to a wire rack to cool, then repeat with the remaining turnovers.

When completely cool, whip the cream with the vanilla extract and sugar, until it forms soft peaks. Use a knife to carefully split open the cooled turnovers like a clam and pipe or spoon the cream inside. Dust with icing sugar and serve.

INDEX

GLOSSARY

UK	US
Aubergine	Eggplant
Baking paper	Parchment paper
Beetroot	Beet
Bicarbonate of soda	Baking soda
Black bean	Turtle bean
Butter bean	Lima bean
Chickpea	Garbanzo bean
Chips (potato)	Fries (potato)
Clingfilm	Plastic wrap
Cocktail stick	Toothpick
Coriander (fresh)	Cilantro
Cornflour	Cornstarch
Courgette	Zucchini
Crisps	Chips
Crumble (fruit)	Crisp
Dark chocolate	Semi-sweet chocolate
Desiccated coconut	Shredded coconut
Double cream	Heavy cream
Dried chilli flakes	Crushed red pepper flakes
Electric whisk	Electric beaters
Flaked almonds	Slivered almonds
Flour, plain/self-raising/wholemeal	Flour, all-purpose/self-rising/wholewheat
Floury potatoes	Baking potatoes
Foil	Aluminium foil
Frying pan	Skillet
Ginger biscuits	Ginger snaps
Golden syrup	Light corn syrup
Grated	Shredded
Ground almonds	Almond meal
Grill	Broil
Icing	Frosting
Jam	Preserves
Jug	Pitcher
Kitchen paper	Paper towel
Mature cheese	Sharp cheese
Measuring jug	Measuring cup

UK	US
Mixed spice	Pie spice mix
Muesli	Granola
Natural yogurt	Plain yogurt
Pak choi	Bok choy
Paper muffin cases	Paper muffin liners
Pepper (red, yellow)	Bell pepper
Porridge oats	Rolled oats
Pudding tin	Baking mould
Pulses	Legumes
Rocket	Arugula
Salad leaves	Greens
Scone	Biscuit
Shortcrust pastry	Basic pie dough
Spring onion	Scallion
Stem ginger	Preserved ginger
Stock	Broth
Suet, vegetable	Shortening, vegetable
Sugar, caster/icing	Sugar, superfine/confectioners'
Sultanas	Golden raisins
Tea towel	Cloth kitchen towel
Tenderstem broccoli	Long-stem broccoli/broccolini
Tomato purée	Tomato paste

ACKNOWLEDGEMENTS

Commissioning Editor: Louisa Johnson
Art Director: Jaz Bahra
Editor: Scarlet Furness
Copyeditor: Jo Smith
Photographer: William Shaw
Food Stylist: Denise Smart
Prop Stylist: Kim Sullivan
Production Controller: Lisa Pinnell
Picture Researcher: Giulia Hetherington

Photography copyright © Octopus Publishing Group/William Shaw